Teaching of The 10 Sikh
MS Chadha

INTRO

Welcome to "Teachings of the 10 Sikh Gurus" interactive journey designed especially for young minds. In this black and white version of our colorful book, we invite kids to embark on a delightful adventure through the teachings of the 10 Sikh Gurus in a way that's both fun and educational.

Why "Teachings of the 10 Sikh Gurus" Lite?
Learning about Sikhism has never been this engaging! We've packed this Lite version with entertaining activities that will not only teach kids about Sikhism but also encourage them to enjoy the process.

🎨 **45+ Coloring Pages:** Unleash your creativity as you color in beautiful illustrations of Sikh Gurus and their stories. It's not just coloring; it's a colorful journey into Sikh history.

🧩 **Fill-in-the-Blanks:** Test your knowledge and memory as you complete sentences about Sikh Gurus and their teachings. It's a fun challenge that lets you actively participate in the learning process.

❓ **Trivia Time:** Get ready for some exciting Sikhism trivia! Learn fascinating facts about Sikh Gurus and their contributions. Impress your friends and family with your newfound knowledge.

🎨 **Draw Your Favourite Guru:** It's not just about coloring; it's about creating! Unleash your artistic side as you draw your favorite Sikh Guru. Express yourself and showcase your talent.

Learning Can Be Fun:
At "Teachings of the 10 Sikh Gurus" Lite, we believe that learning should be enjoyable. We've designed this Lite version to make Sikhism come alive for kids. It's not just a book; it's a journey of discovery, creativity, and inspiration.

By actively participating in the learning process, kids will not only gain a deeper understanding of Sikhism but also develop a strong connection with its teachings. We want young minds to be excited about Sikh history, to be inspired by the wisdom of the Gurus, and to enjoy every moment of this enriching experience.

So, are you ready to dive into a world of colors, puzzles, trivia, and creativity while learning about Sikhism? Let's embark on this wonderful journey together!

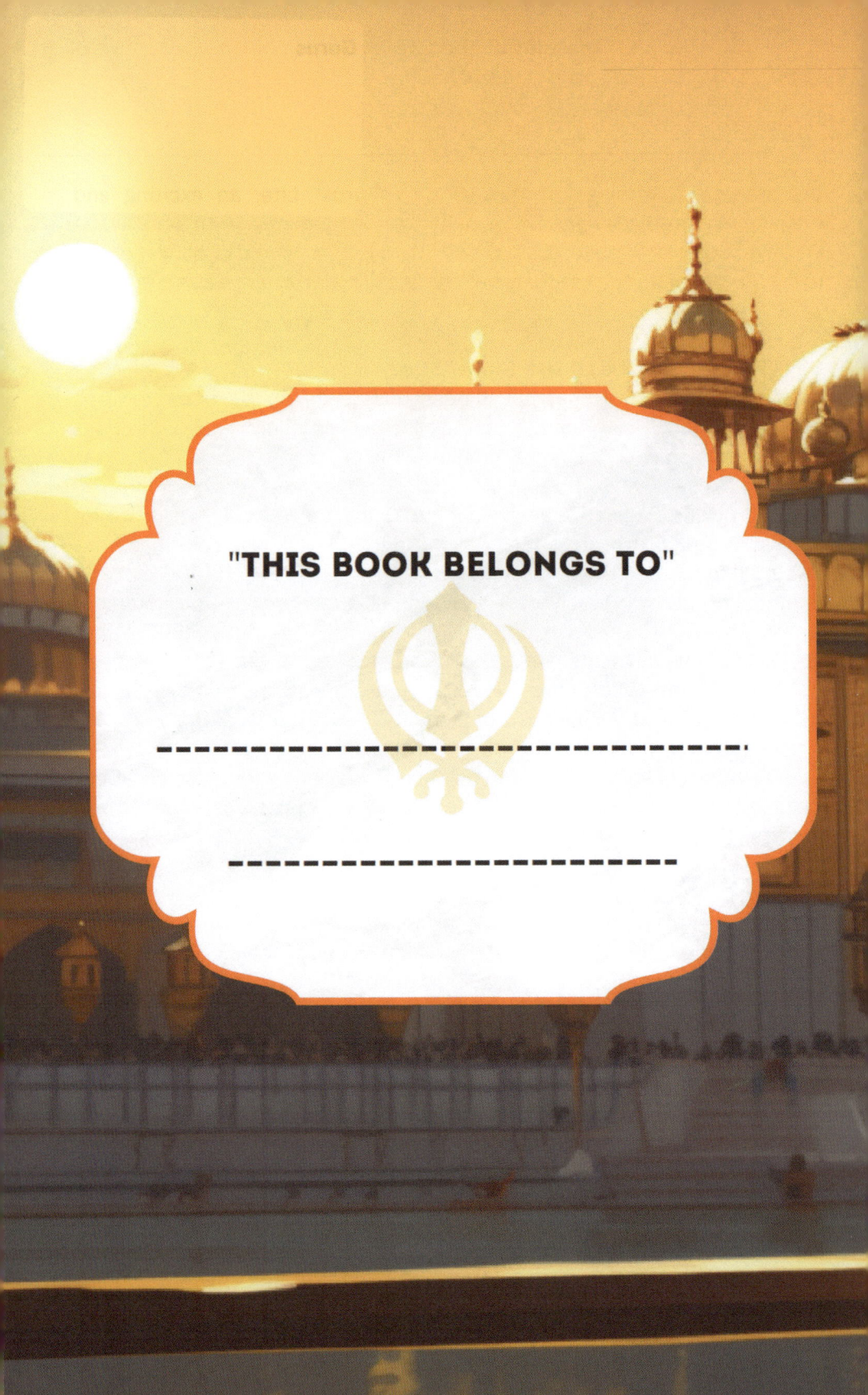

TEACHINGS OF THE 10 SIKH GURUS

In this enchanting children's book, we embark on an extraordinary journey to explore the timeless wisdom and teachings of the 10 Sikh Gurus.

"UNLOCK THE HIDDEN WISDOM"

In the spirit of unity and understanding, we will encounter the beautiful Sikh way of life and the timeless message of treating every soul with kindness and respect. Through these pages, young minds will be inspired.

INTRODUCTION TO SIKHISM

Welcome to the fascinating world of Sikhism, a religion founded on the principles of love, equality, and selfless service. If you are new to Sikhism, let this page be your gateway to understanding teachings of this faith.

Sikhism was born in the 15th century in the Punjab region of South Asia, under the divine guidance of Guru Nanak Dev Ji, the first of the ten Sikh Gurus.

At its core, Sikhism believes in the oneness of the Supreme Being and the equality of all human beings, irrespective of their caste, creed, or gender.

Sikhs, the followers of Sikhism, are recognized by their distinctive appearance, including the turban and the uncut hair, symbolizing their commitment to the faith's principles of honesty, righteousness, and courage.

As you delve into the stories of the ten Sikh Gurus and their timeless wisdom, you will discover the essence of Sikhism - a path that leads to spiritual enlightenment, inner peace, and a life of service to others.

Join us on this enlightening journey, and let the teachings of Sikhism touch your heart and enrich your soul.

WAHEGURU JI KA KHALSA, WAHEGURU JI KI FATEH!

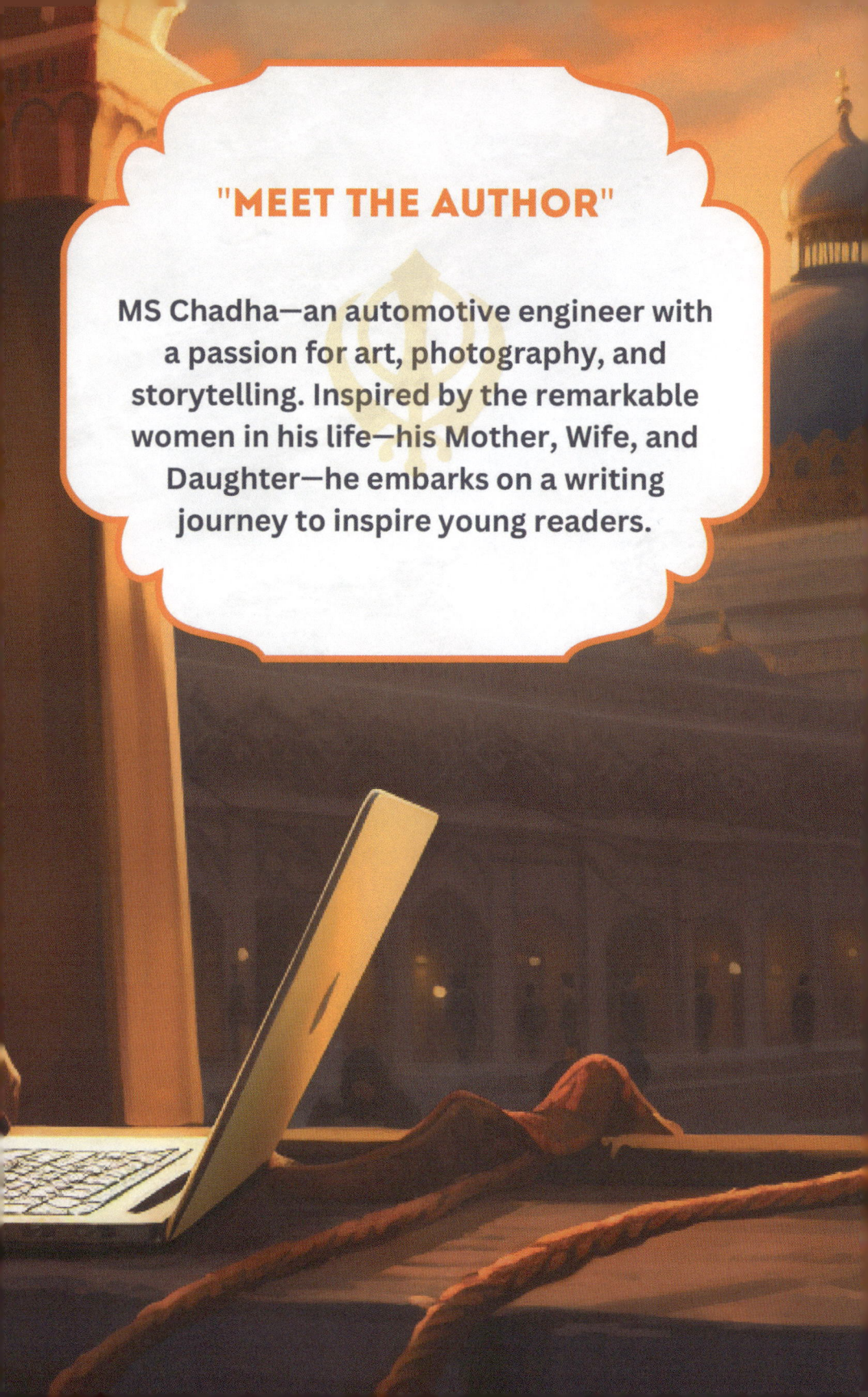

"MEET THE AUTHOR"

MS Chadha—an automotive engineer with a passion for art, photography, and storytelling. Inspired by the remarkable women in his life—his Mother, Wife, and Daughter—he embarks on a writing journey to inspire young readers.

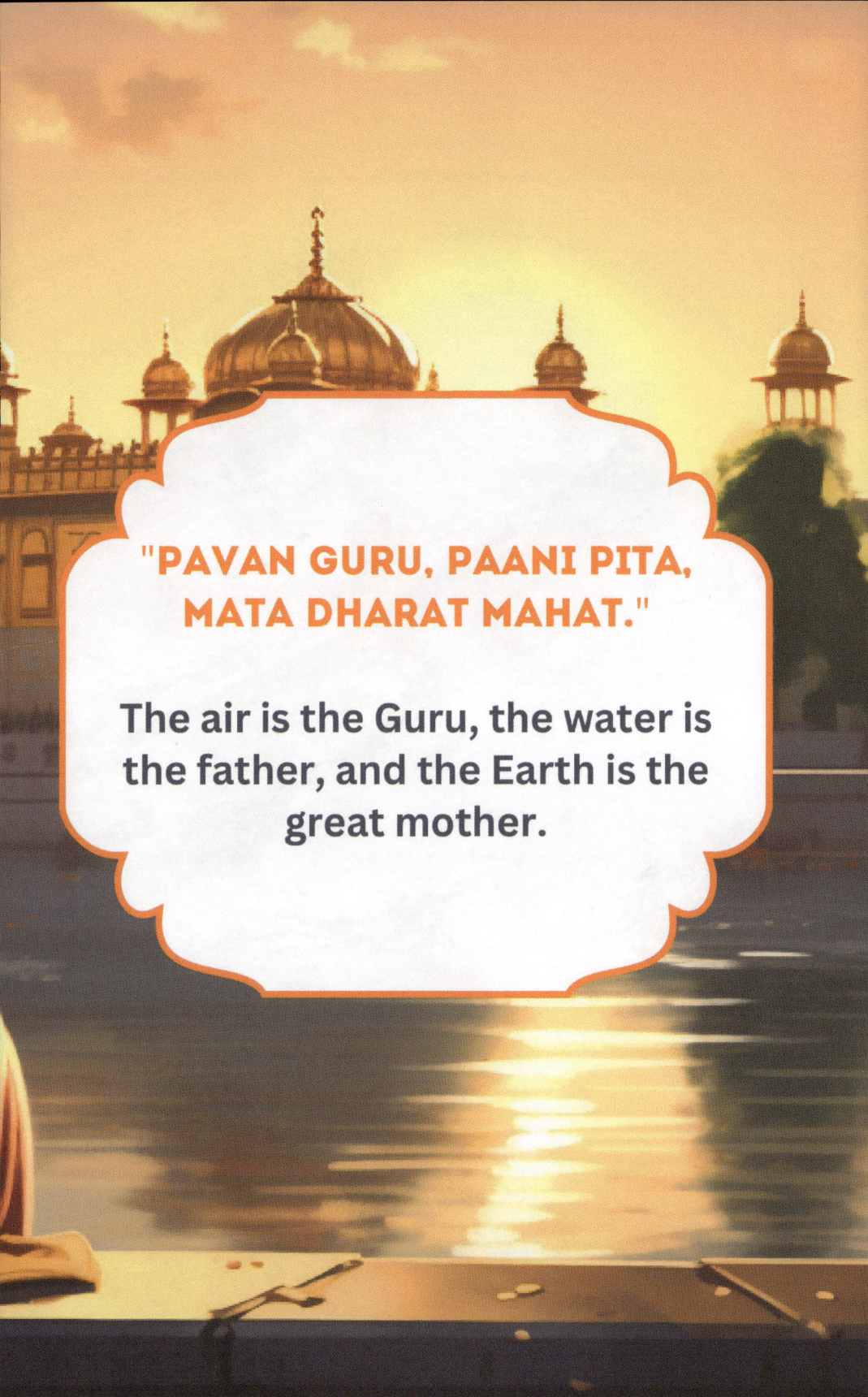

"PAVAN GURU, PAANI PITA, MATA DHARAT MAHAT."

The air is the Guru, the water is the father, and the Earth is the great mother.

GURU NANAK DEV JI

Place of Birth: Nankana Sahib, Pakistan

Life Span: 1469-1539
Became Guru at the age of 30.

Father: Mehta Kalu
Mother: Mata Tripta

Interesting Fact:
Guru Nanak Dev Ji travelled to different parts of India, the Middle East, and Asia to spread his message of love, equality, and devotion to God.

Teaching:

"Treat all as equals, for we are all children of the same Divine Light."

ਇੱਕ ਓਅੰਕਾਰ

"IK ONKAR"

There is only one God and creator.

GURU ANGAD DEV JI

Place of Birth: Matte Di Sarai, Pakistan

Life Span: 1504-1552
Became Guru at the age of 35.

Father: Baba Pheru
Mother: Mata Ramo

Interesting Fact: Guru Angad Dev Ji introduced the Gurmukhi script, which became the written form of Punjabi and is now the script used to write the Sikh scriptures and literature.

Teaching:

"Seek knowledge as a lamp that illuminates the path of wisdom."

ਗੁਰ ਸਤਿਗੁਰ ਕਾ ਜੋ ਸਿਖੁ ਅਖਾਵੈ

"GUR SATGUR KA JO SIKH AKHAVE"

Be a true student and learn from the wisdom of the Guru.

GURU AMAR DAS JI

Place of Birth: Basarke, India

Life Span: 1479-1574
Became Guru at the age of 73.

Father: Tej Bhan Bhalla
Mother: Mata Bakht

Interesting Fact: Guru Amar Das Ji institutionalized the concept of the Langar, a community kitchen where people of all backgrounds and castes could sit together and share a meal, promoting equality and breaking social barriers.

Teaching:

"Break the barriers of caste and embrace the oneness of humanity."

ਮੇਰਾ ਮੁਝ ਮੈਂ ਕਿਛੁ ਨਹੀਂ

"MERA MUJH MEIN KICHH NAHIN"

Realize that everything belongs to the Divine, and practice selflessness.

GURU RAM DAS JI

Place of Birth: Lahore, Pakistan

Life Span: 1534-1581
Became Guru at the age of 40.

Father: Baba Hari Das
Mother: Mata Daya Vati

Interesting Fact: Guru Ram Das Ji founded the city of Amritsar, where he established the Harmandir Sahib, famously known as the Golden Temple, which is the most sacred shrine in Sikhism.

Teaching:

"Embrace the divine light within and let it illuminate your path."

ਆਪੇ ਗੁਰ ਚੇਲਾ

"AAPE GUR CHELA"

Recognize the Guru's presence within yourself and surrender to the divine guidance.

GURU ARJAN DEV JI

Place of Birth: Goindval, India

Life Span: 1563-1606
Became Guru at the age of 18.

Father: Rām Dās
Mother: Mata Bhani

Interesting Fact: Guru Arjan Dev Ji compiled and installed the Adi Granth, the Sikh scripture, and completed the construction of the Harmandir Sahib.

Teaching:

"Recognize the divine light in every being and embrace the spirit of oneness.

ਬਾਣੀ ਗੁਰੂ, ਗੁਰੂ ਹੈ ਬਾਣੀ

"BANI GURU, GURU HAI BANI"

Seek guidance from the divine teachings and let them be your Guru.

GURU HARGOBIND JI

Place of Birth: Wadali, Pakistan

Life Span: 1595-1644
Became Guru at the age of 11.

Father: Arjun Dēv
Mother: Mata Ganga

Interesting Fact: Guru Hargobind Ji introduced the concept of Miri-Piri, emphasizing the balance between spiritual and temporal matters. He wore two swords, symbolizing his dual responsibility as a spiritual leader and a warrior.

Teaching:

"Embrace the path of righteousness and stand against injustice."

ਦੇਹ ਸਿਵਾ ਬਰ ਮੋਹੇ ਈਹੇ

"DEH SHIVA BAR MOHE EHE"

Seek divine strength to fight for justice and protect the innocent.

7.
GURU HAR RAI JI

Place of Birth: Kiratpur, India

Life Span: 1630-1661
Became Guru at the age of 14.

Father: Baba Gurditta
Mother: Mata Nihal

Interesting Fact: Guru Har Rai Ji was known for his love for nature and animals. He maintained a medicinal garden and a zoo in Kiratpur, nurturing a deep connection between humans and the environment.

Teaching:

"Spread love and compassion to all living beings, for we are part of the divine creation.

ਜਿਨ ਪ੍ਰੇਮ ਕਿਓ ਤਿਨ ਹੀ ਪ੍ਰਭ ਪਾਇਓ

"JIN PREM KIYO TIN HI PRABH PAYO"

Embrace the power of love, for it leads to the realization of the divine presence.

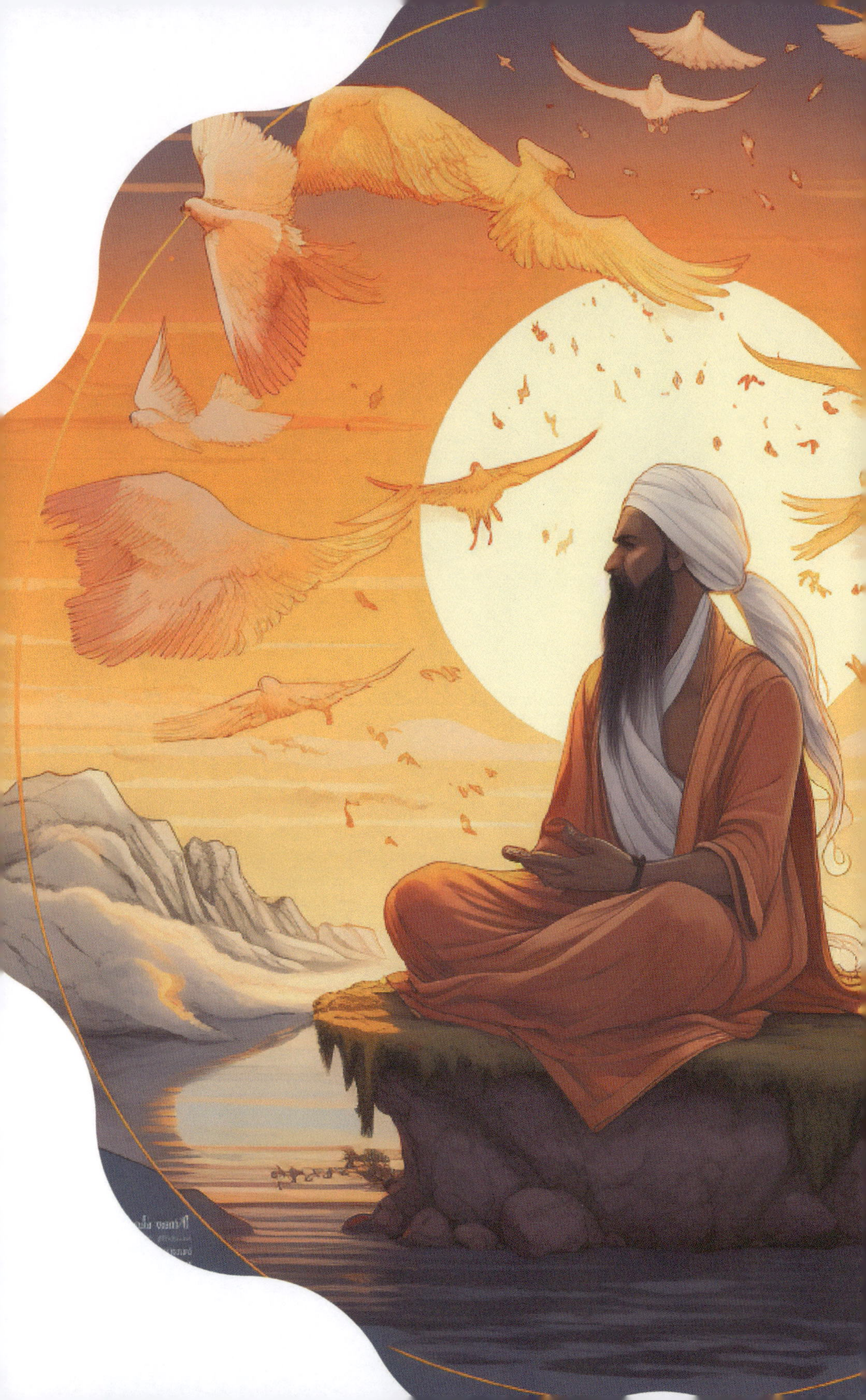

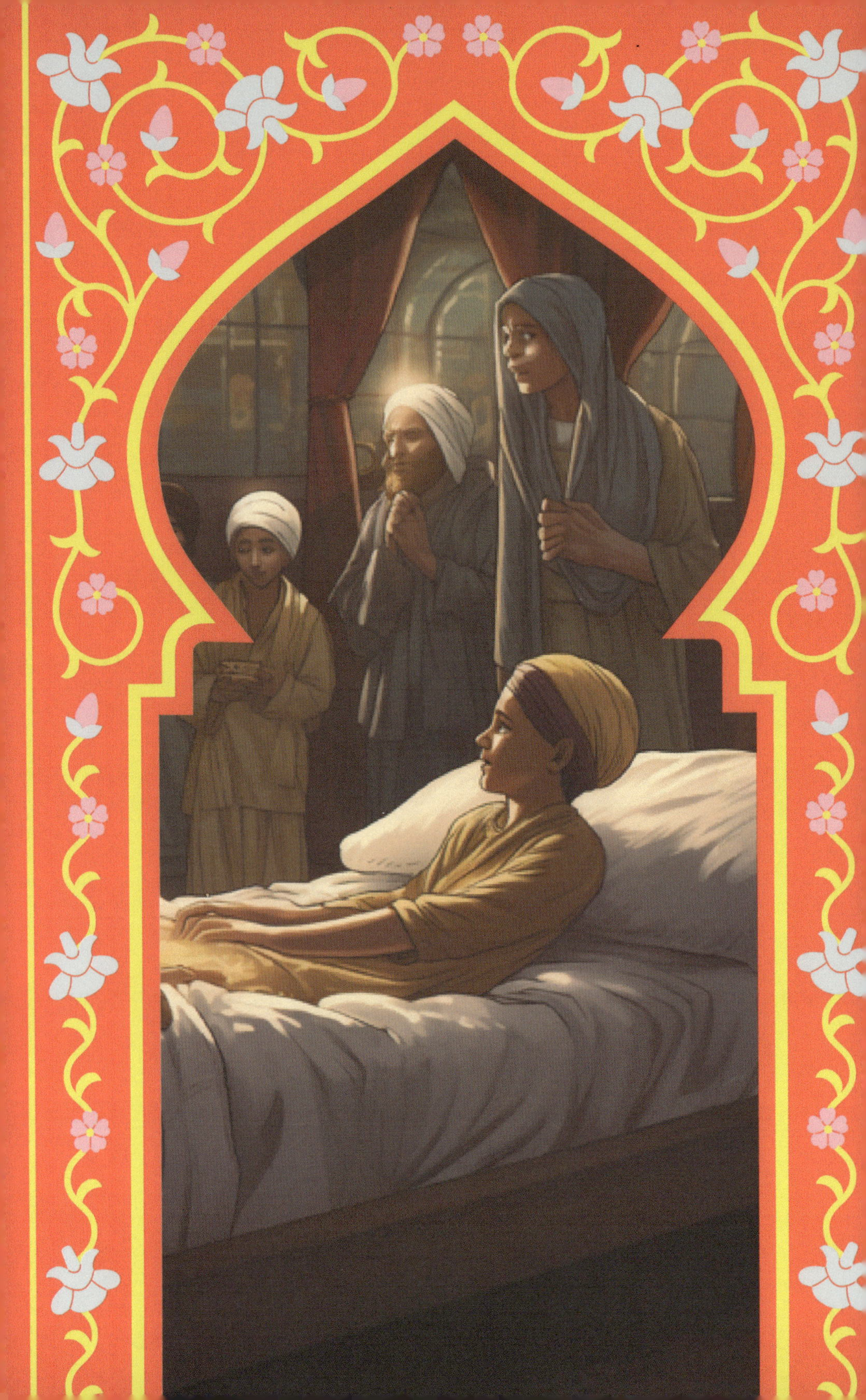

8.
GURU HAR KRISHAN JI

Place of Birth: Kiratpur, India

Life Span: 1656-1664
Became Guru at the age of 5.

Father: Hari Rā'i
Mother: Mata Krishan

Interesting Fact: Guru Har Krishan Ji became the youngest Guru at the age of five. Despite his short life, he showed great compassion and selflessness, dedicating himself to healing the sick during a smallpox epidemic in Delhi.

Teaching:

"Serve others with a selfless heart, and bring comfort to the suffering."

ਜੋਤ ਰੂਪ ਹਰਿ ਆਪੁ ਗੁਰੂ ਨਾਨਕ ਕਹਾਏਓ

"JOT ROOP HAR AAP GURU NANAK KAHAYEO"

Recognize the divine presence within every Guru, for they are the embodiment of eternal wisdom.

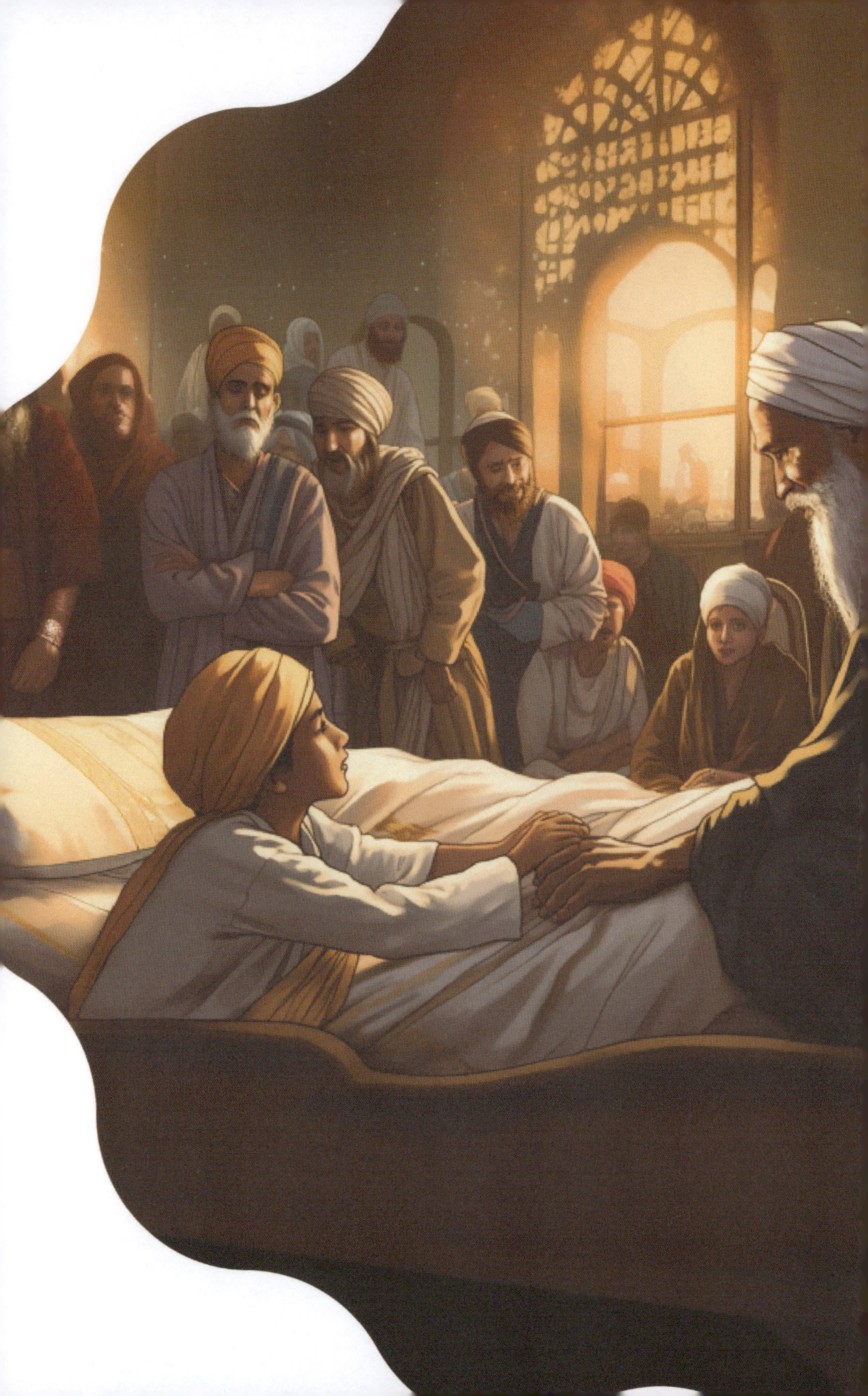

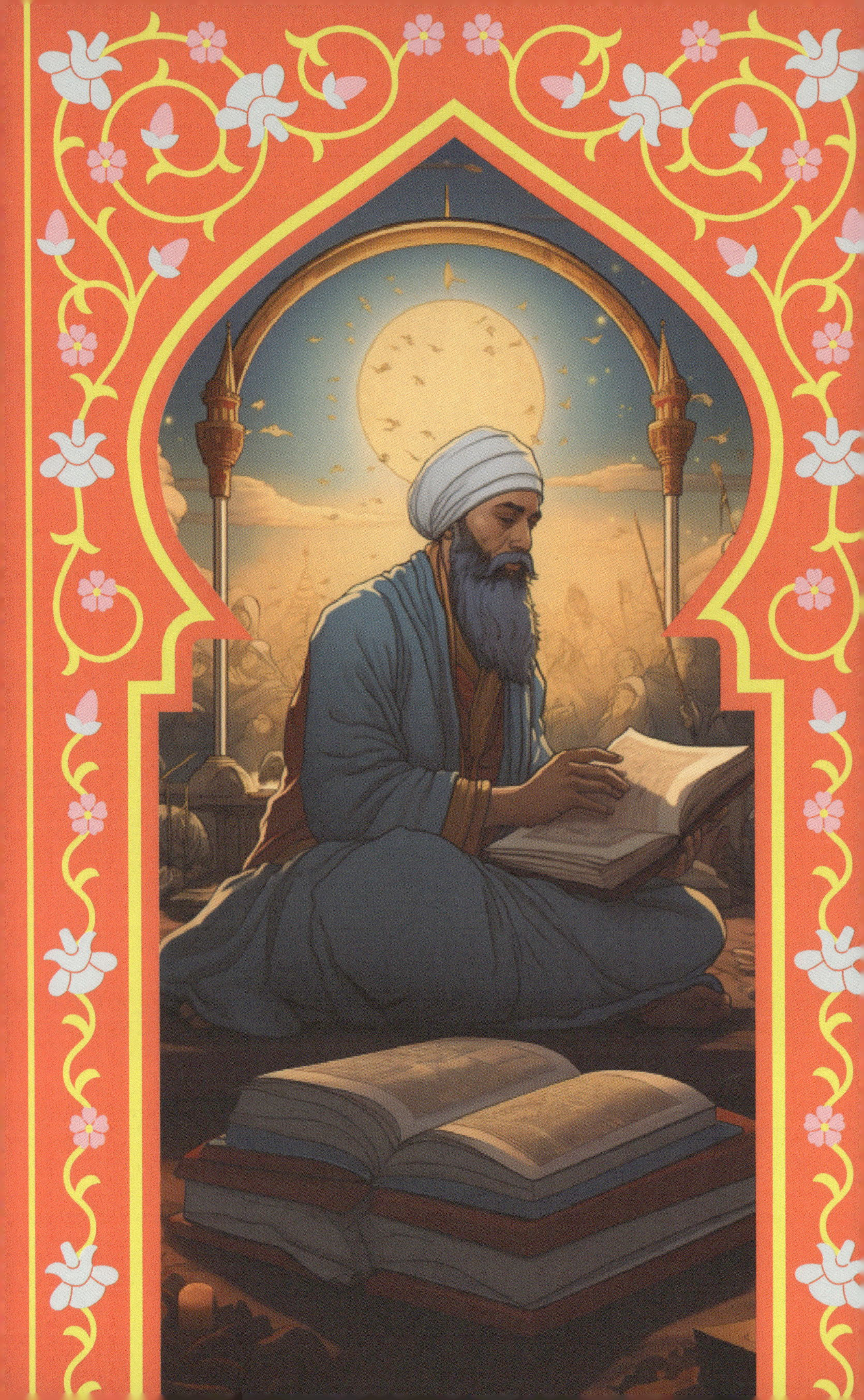

9.
GURU TEGH BAHADUR JI

Place of Birth: Amritsar, India

Life Span: 1621-1675
Became Guru at the age of 43.

Father: Hari Gōbind
Mother: Mata Nanki

Interesting Fact: Guru Tegh Bahadur Ji sacrificed his life to protect the religious freedom of Hindus when they faced persecution under the Mughal Empire. He is known as "Hind Di Chadar," the Shield of India.

Teaching:

"Stand for the freedom of religion and protect the rights of all people."

ਸਭਨਾ ਜੀਆ ਕਾ ਇਕੁ ਦਾਤਾ

"SABHNA JIYA KA IK DAATA"

There is one Creator of all creations.

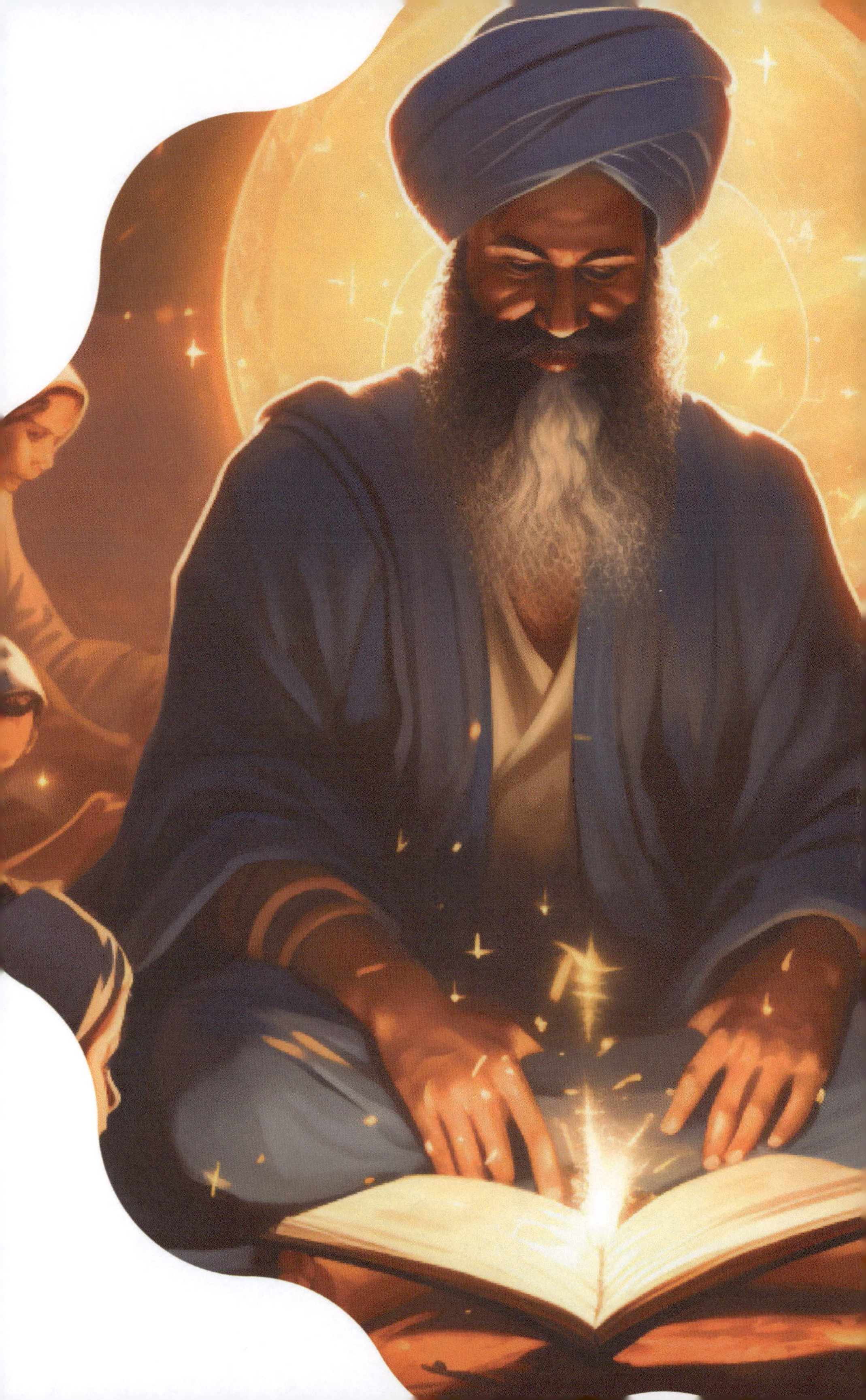

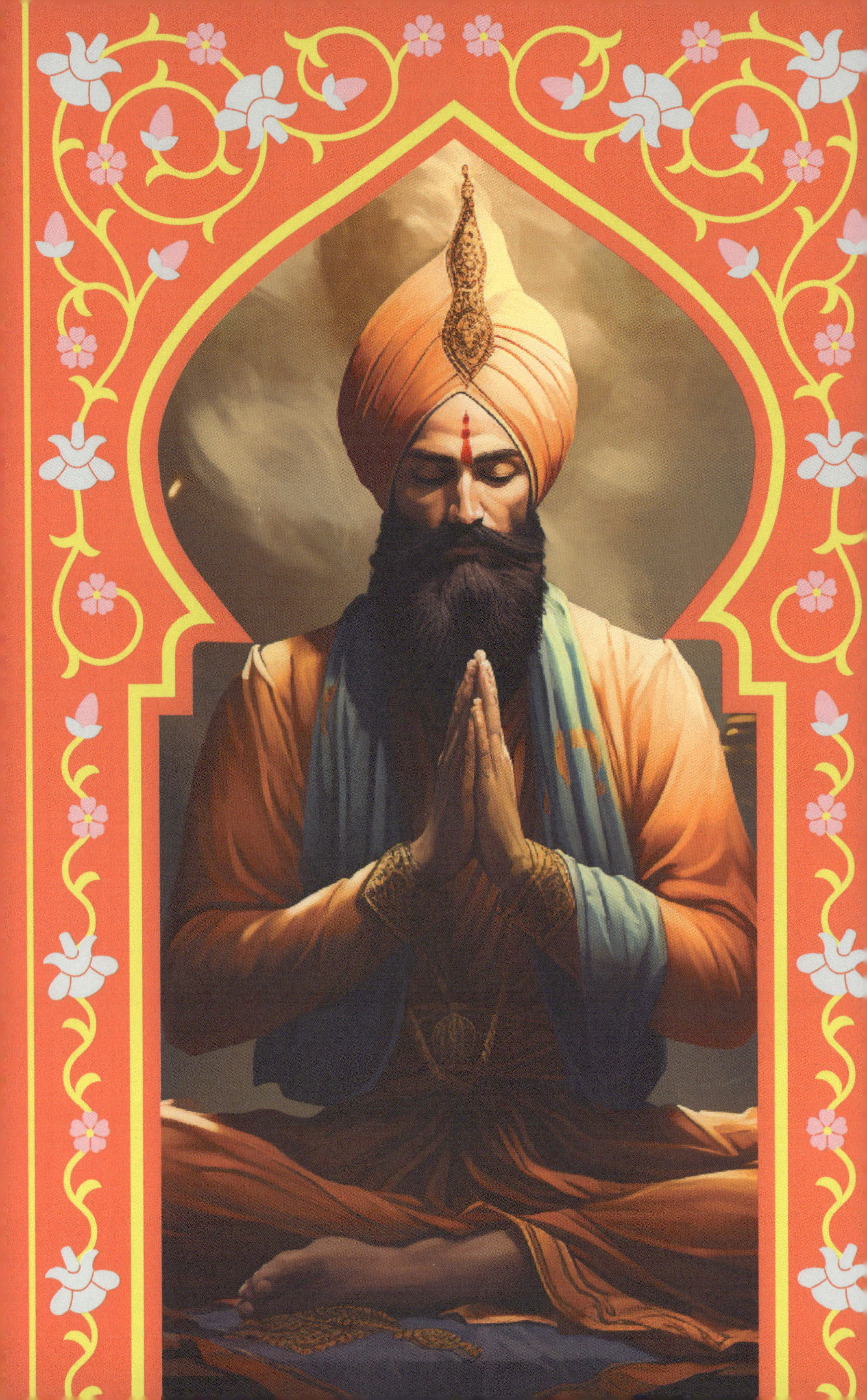

10.
GURU GOBIND SINGH JI

Place of Birth: Patna, present-day India

Life Span: 1666-1708
Became Guru at the age of 9.

Father: Tēġ Bahādur
Mother: Mata Gujri

Interesting Fact: Guru Gobind Singh Ji established the Khalsa, a community of initiated Sikhs, and introduced the Five Ks (Kesh, Kangha, Kara, Kachera, and Kirpan) as symbols of Sikh identity and devotion.

Teaching:

"Embrace the Khalsa spirit and uphold righteousness in all aspects of life."

ਚਿੜੋਂ ਸੇ ਮੈਂ ਬਾਜ਼ ਤੁਰਾਊਂ, ਤਬੇ ਗੋਬਿੰਦ ਸਿੰਘ ਨਾਮ ਕਹਾਊਂ

"CHIRION SE MAIN BAAZ TURAUN, TABE GOBIND SINGH NAAM KAHAUN"

It is when I make sparrows fight hawks that I am called Gobind Singh.

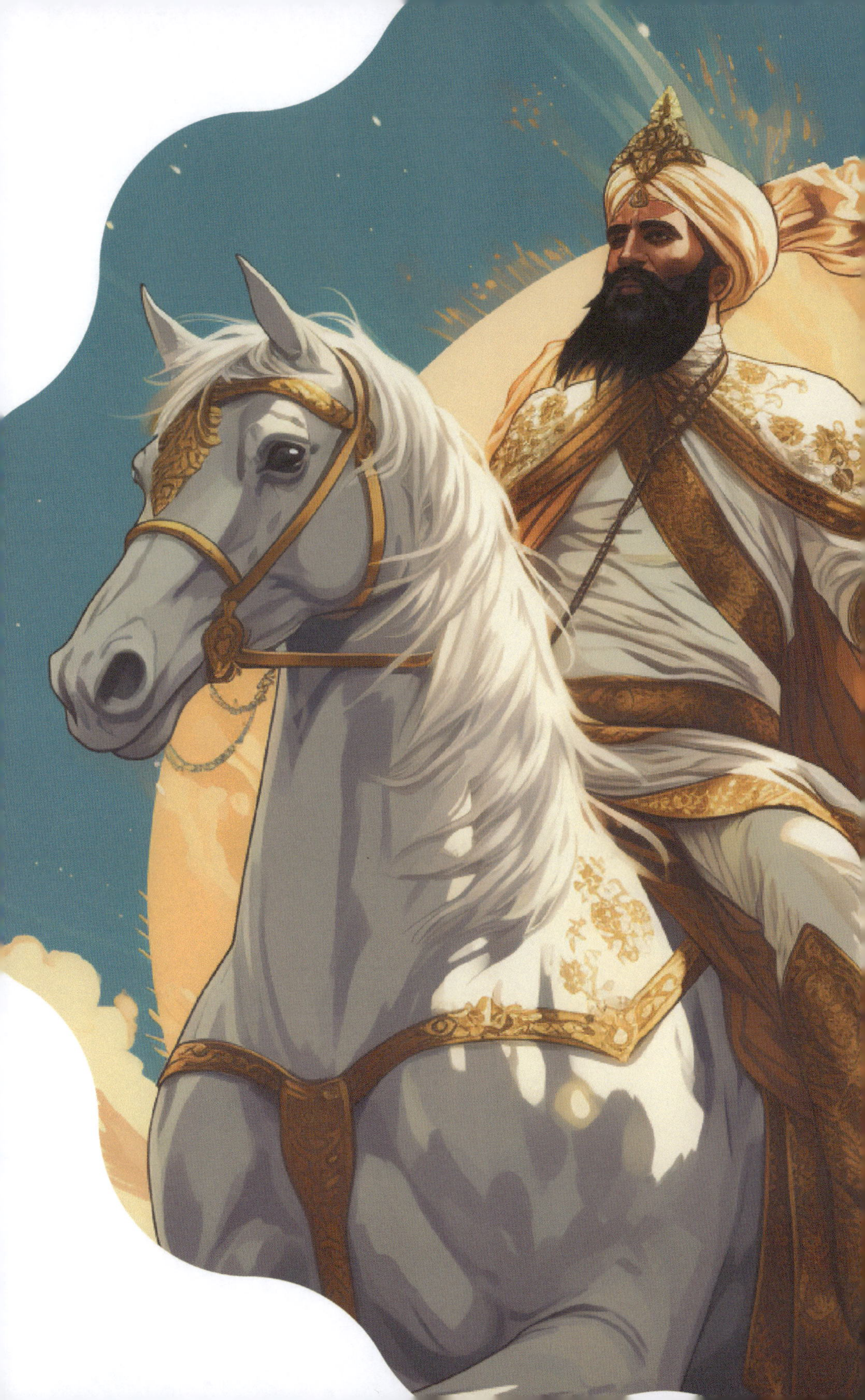

Discovering the Light Within: "The Teachings of the 10 Sikh Gurus"

Illuminate the path of wisdom, compassion, and unity. Through the inspiring lives of the Gurus, children learn the importance of love, equality, and selfless service.

This book instils the moral that by embracing these timeless teachings, we can ignite the divine light within ourselves and radiate it to the world, creating a harmonious and compassionate society for all."

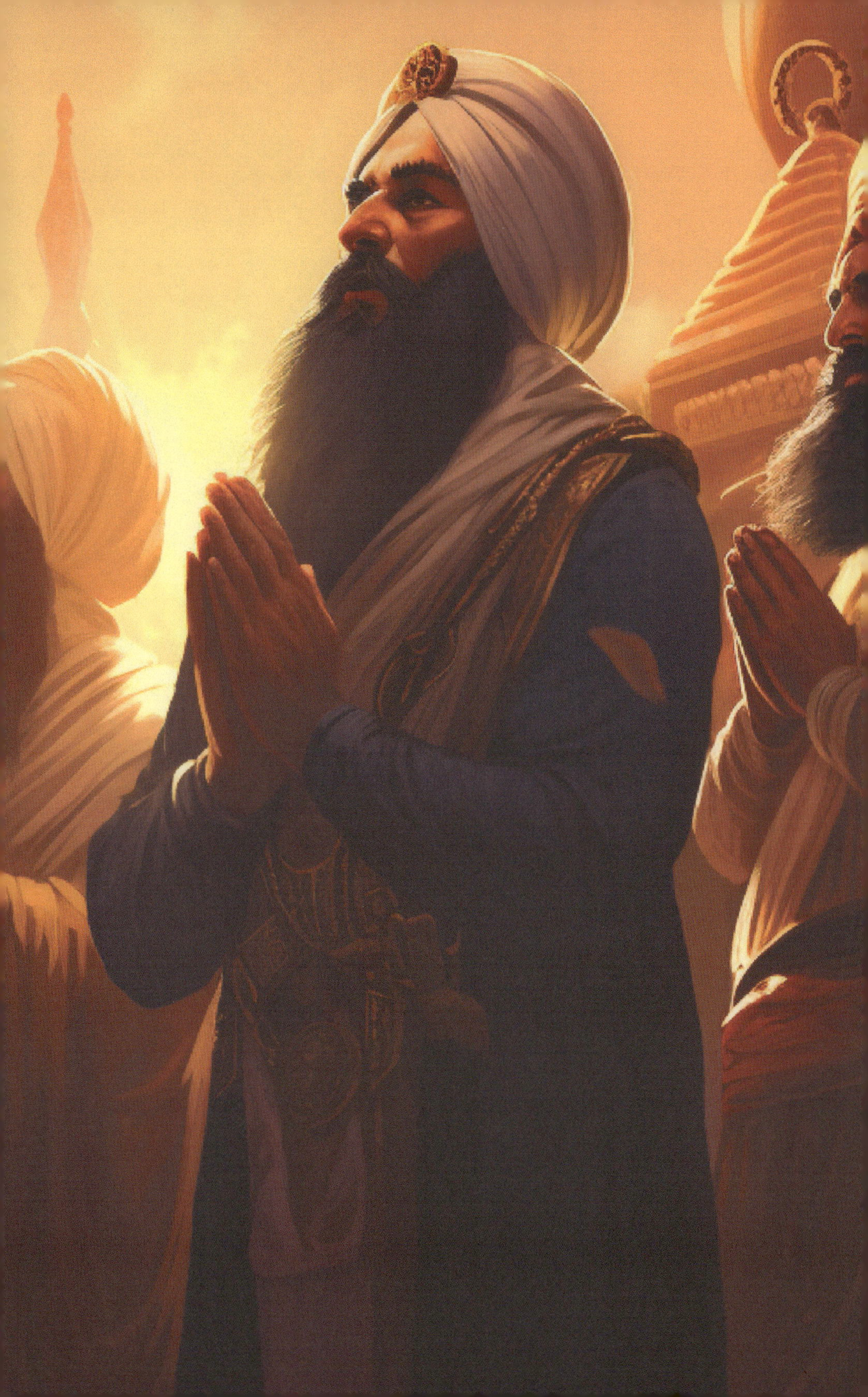

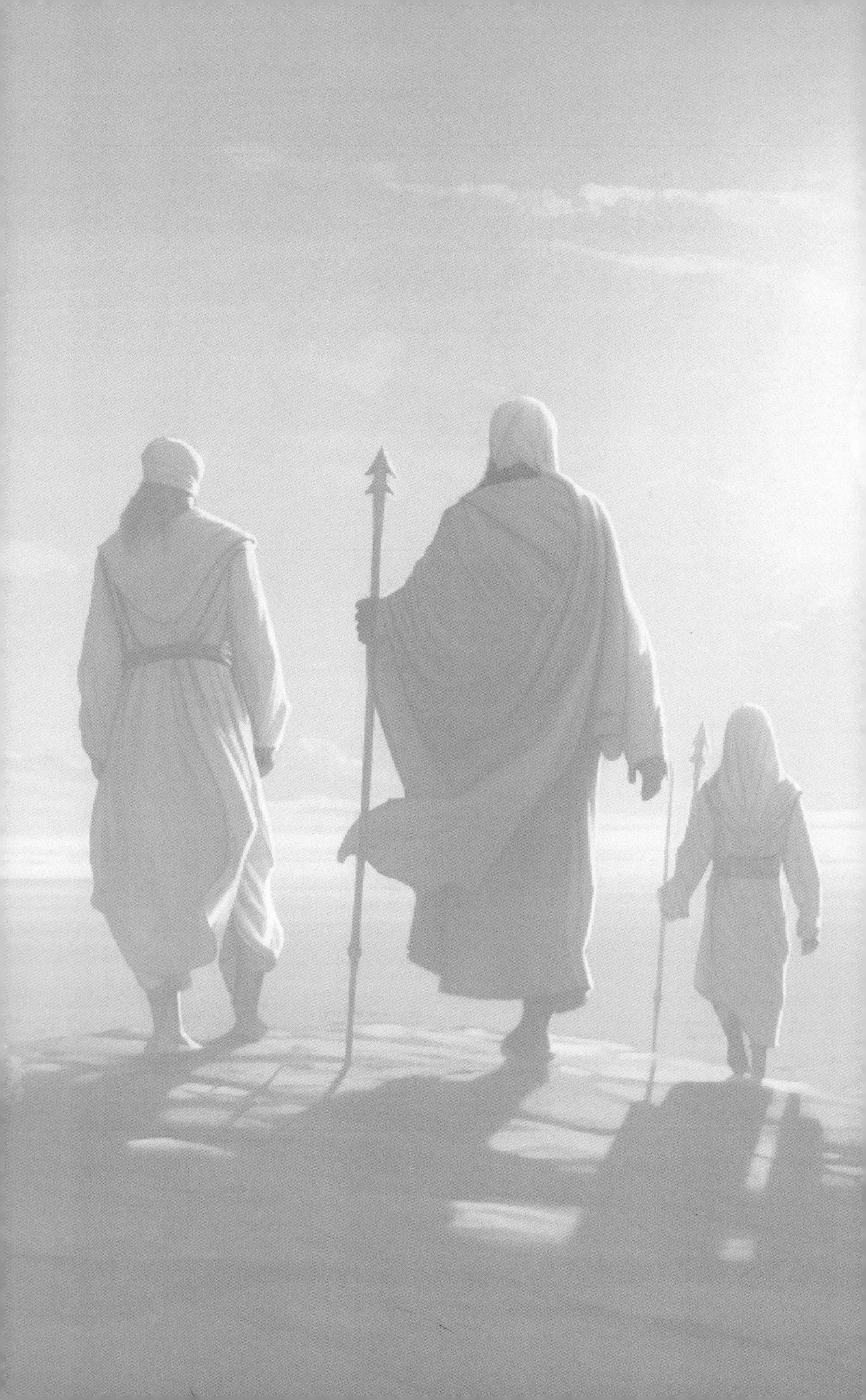

ACTIVITIES:

This book is designed to spark your creativity, challenge your knowledge, and strengthen your bond with the Gurus.

Inside these pages, you'll find a variety of captivating activities that will transport you to the heart of Sikhism.

From colouring images of the Gurus to searching for hidden names in word puzzles, every activity is crafted to make learning both enjoyable and meaningful.

Index:

- Fill-in-the-Blanks
- Trivia
- Colouring Pages: 45+ pages
- Draw Your Favourite Guru

Grab your colours, pens, and imagination, and let's begin this exciting adventure of self-discovery and spiritual wisdom!

FILL-IN THE-BLANKS

GURU NANAK DEV JI'S JOURNEY

Guru Nanak Dev Ji was born in the year _____ in the village of _____.

From a young age, he showed deep _____ and a strong sense of _____.

As he grew older, he embarked on several spiritual _____ to spread the message of love, _____, and unity among people of all _____.

GURU ANGAD DEV JI'S CONTRIBUTIONS

Guru Angad Dev Ji, the second Guru of the Sikhs, played a vital role in _____ the Gurmukhi script.

He also emphasized the importance of _____ and selfless service.

He established the tradition of _____ the Guru's teachings through singing hymns and devotional _____.

Trivia - Test Your Knowledge about Sikh Gurus!

- Who was the founder of Sikhism? Answer: Guru Nanak Dev Ji

- Which Guru compiled the Sikh scriptures into the Guru Granth Sahib? Answer: Guru Arjan Dev Ji

- Which Guru is known for constructing the Golden Temple (Harmandir Sahib)? Answer: Guru Ram Das Ji

- Guru Gobind Singh Ji introduced the Sikh community to the "Five Ks." What are they? Answer: Kesh (uncut hair), Kara (steel bracelet), Kanga (wooden comb), Kachera (undergarment), and Kirpan (ceremonial sword)

- Which Guru emphasized the importance of selfless service through the institution of Langar? Answer: Guru Amar Das Ji

- Who was the ninth Guru of the Sikhs?
  Answer: Guru Tegh Bahadur Ji

- Which Guru initiated the practice of "Pahul," the Sikh baptism ceremony?
  Answer: Guru Gobind Singh Ji

- Which Guru laid the foundation of the city of Amritsar around the Golden Temple?
  Answer: Guru Ram Das Ji

- Which Guru is known for composing hymns that are included in the Guru Granth Sahib? Answer: Guru Angad Dev Ji

- Who was the father of Guru Nanak Dev Ji?
  Answer: Mehta Kalu

- Which Guru is known for standing up against religious persecution and sacrificing his life for the freedom of faith? Answer: Guru Tegh Bahadur Ji

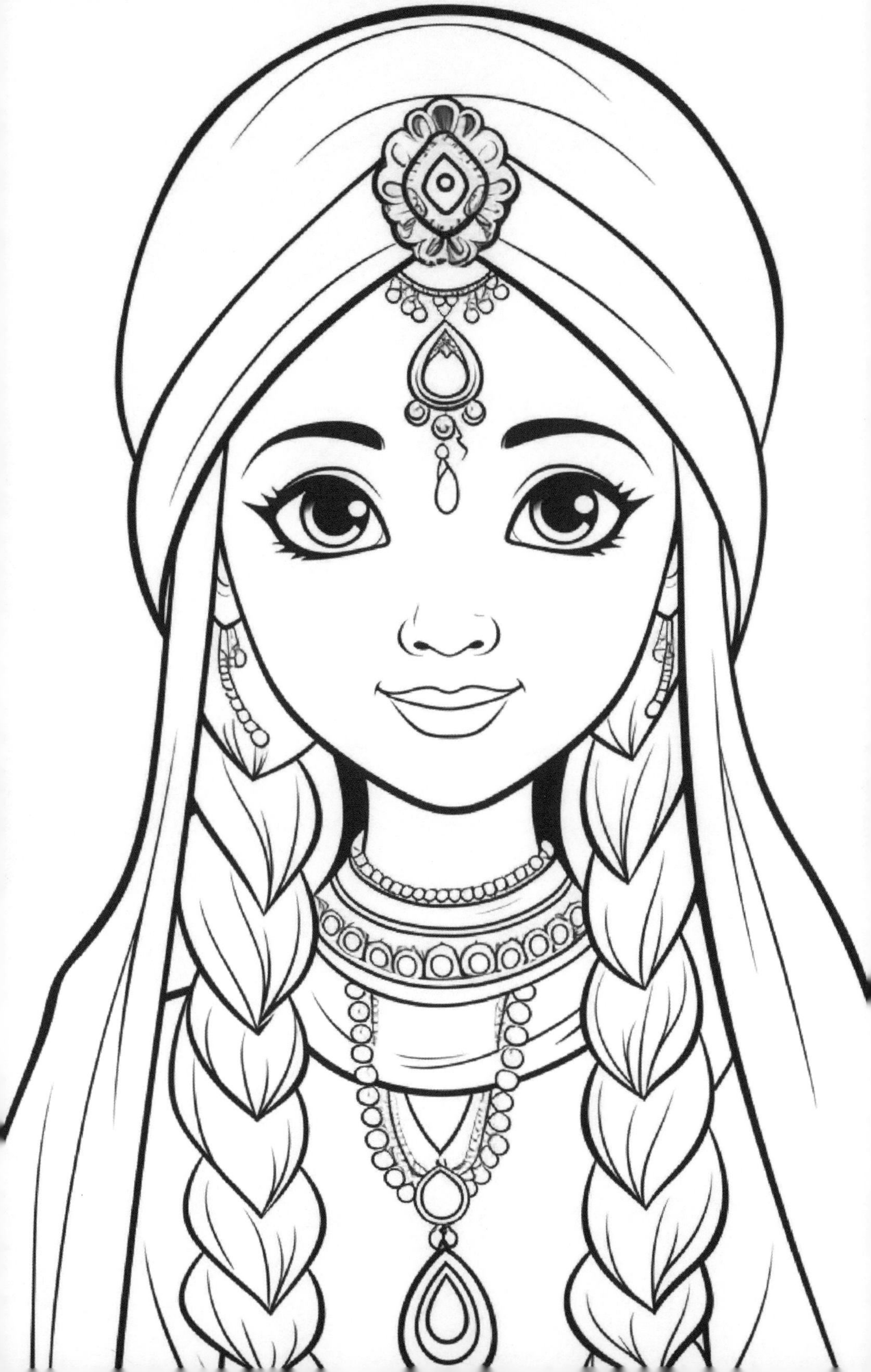

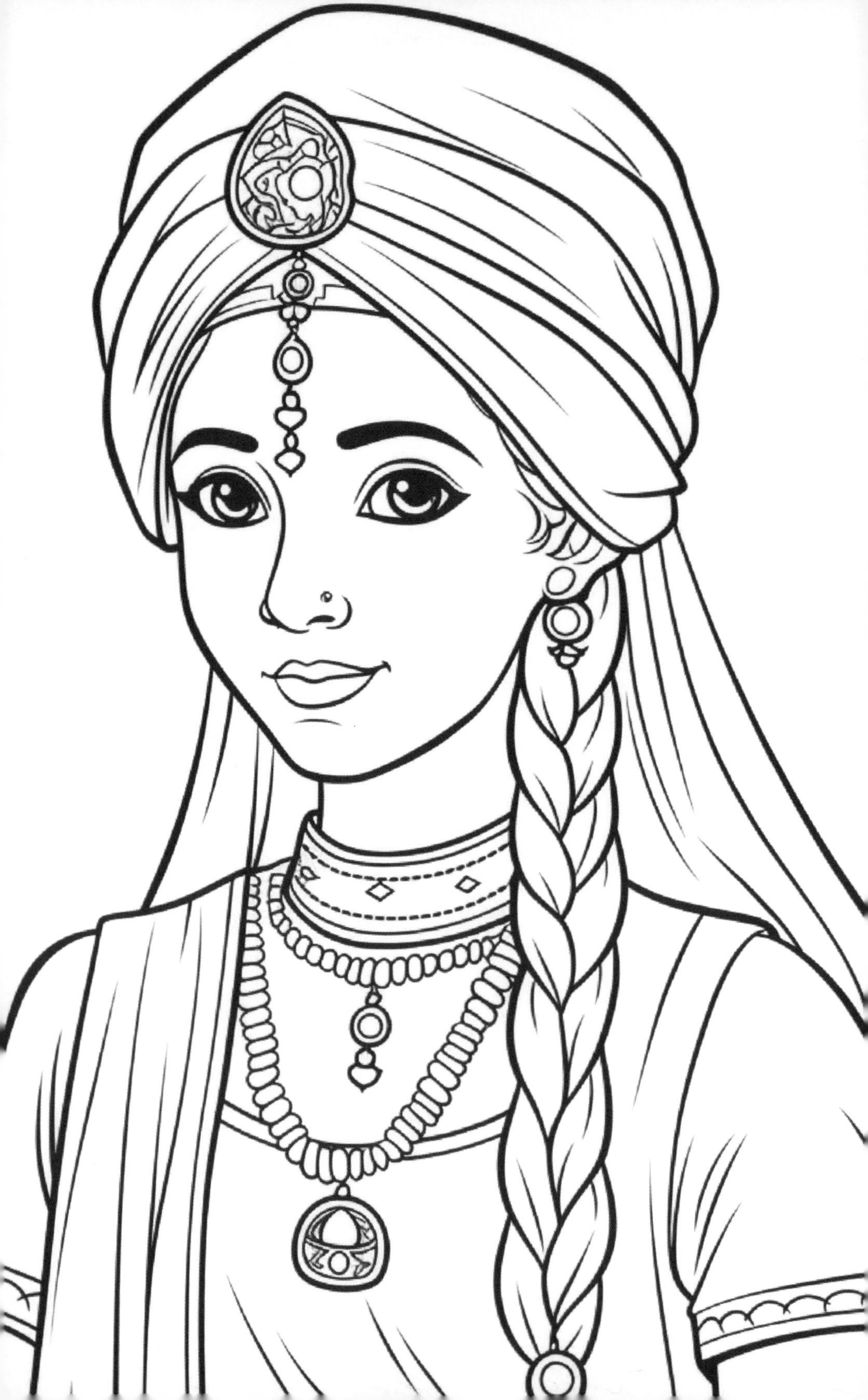

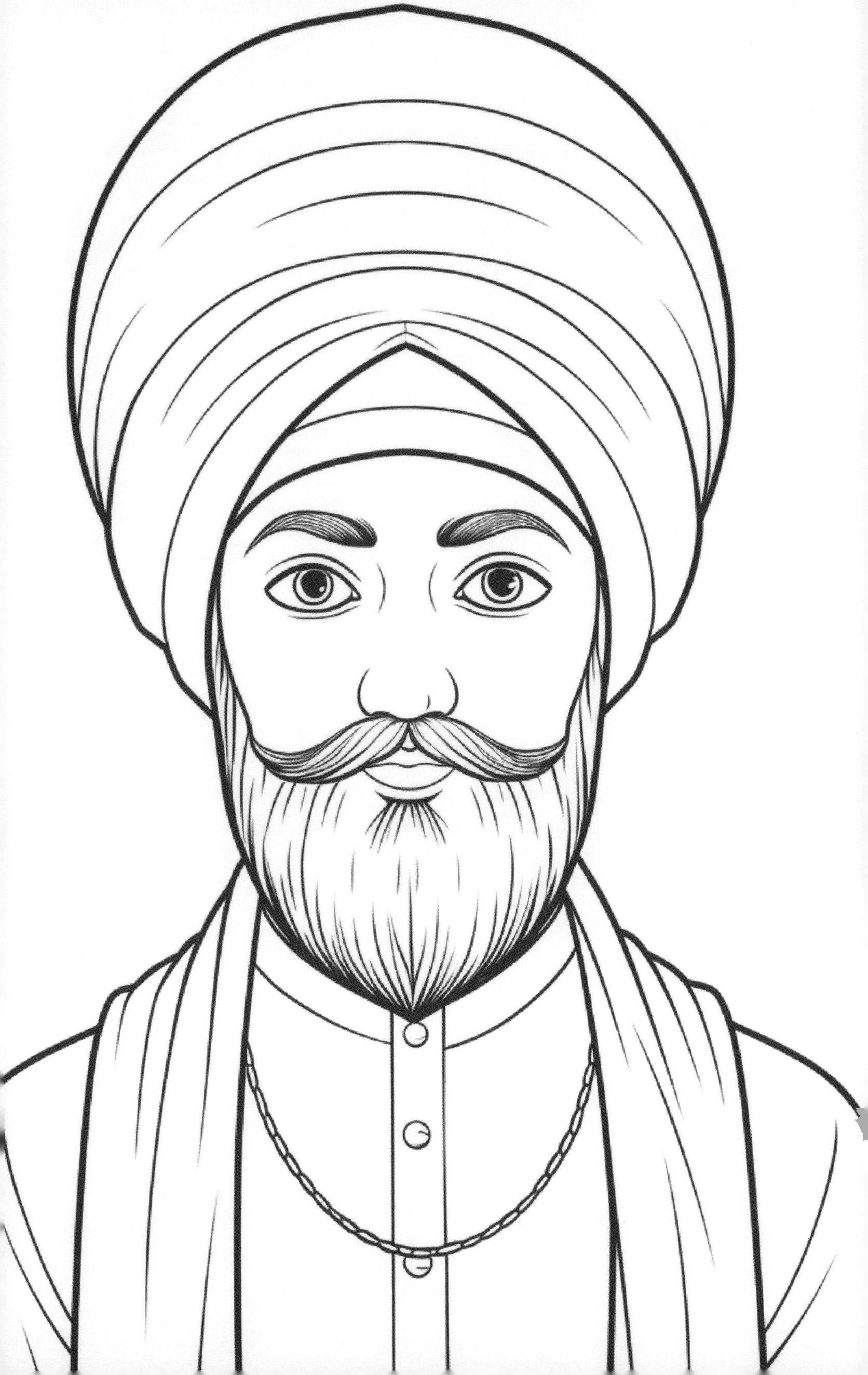

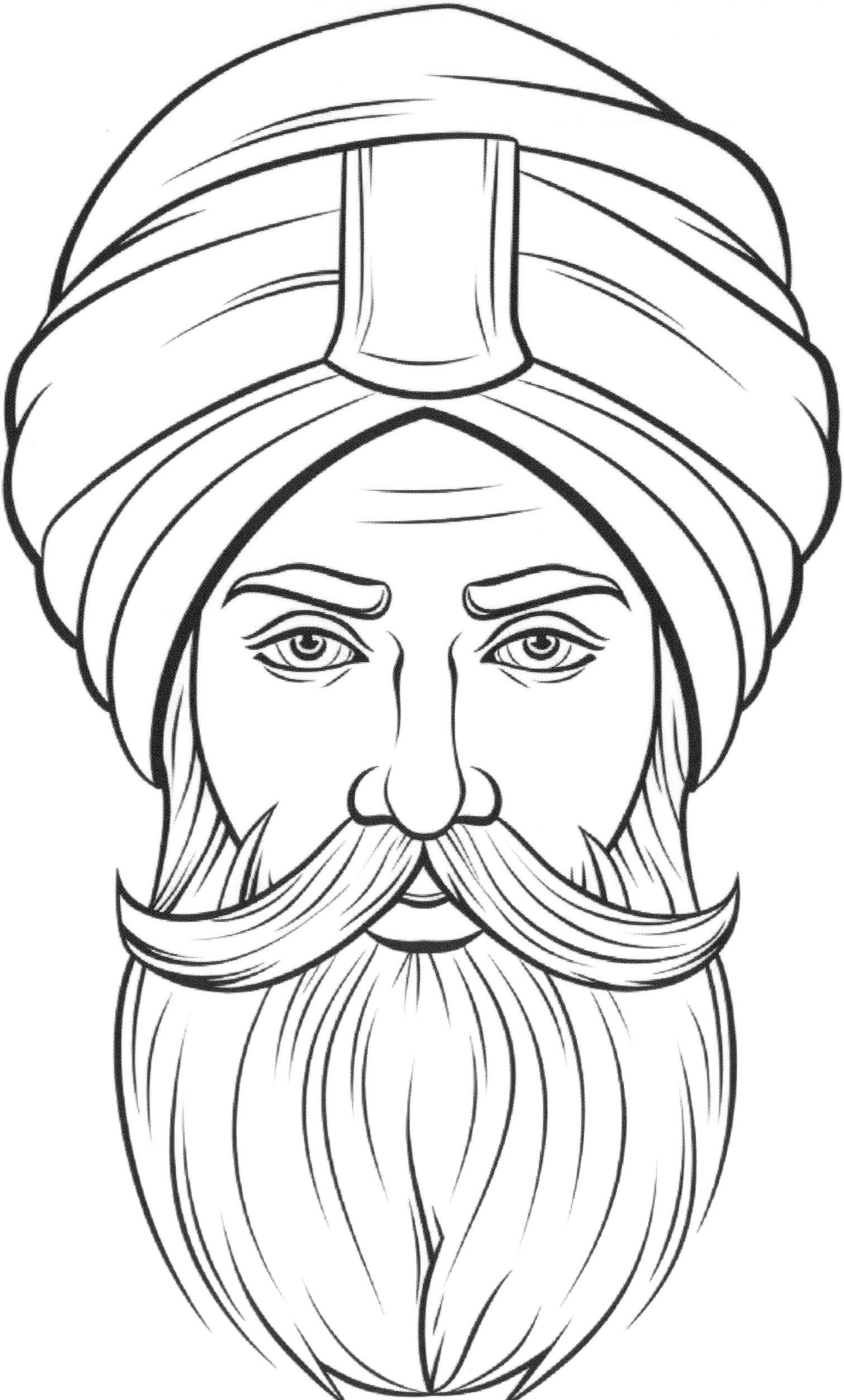

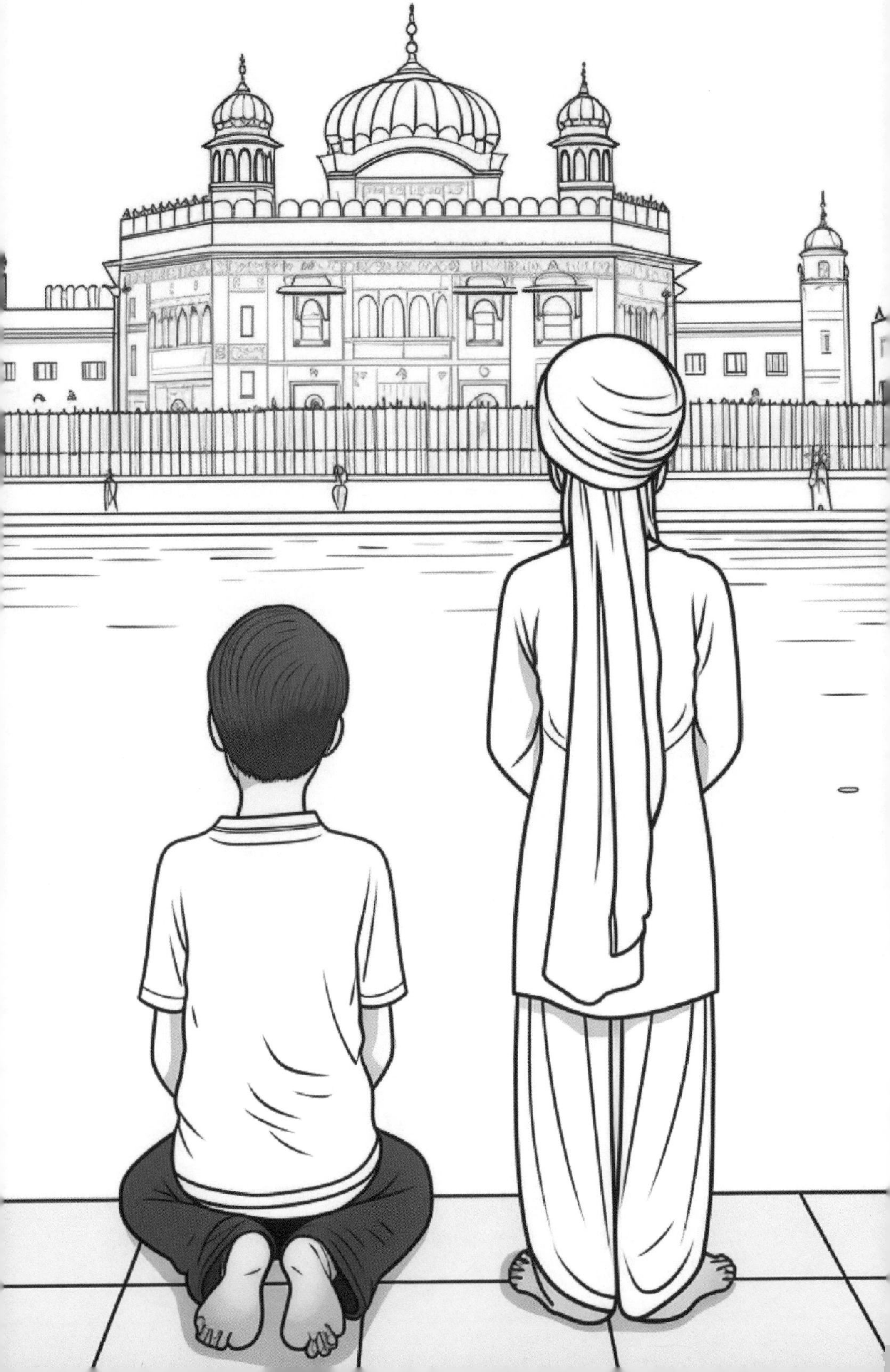

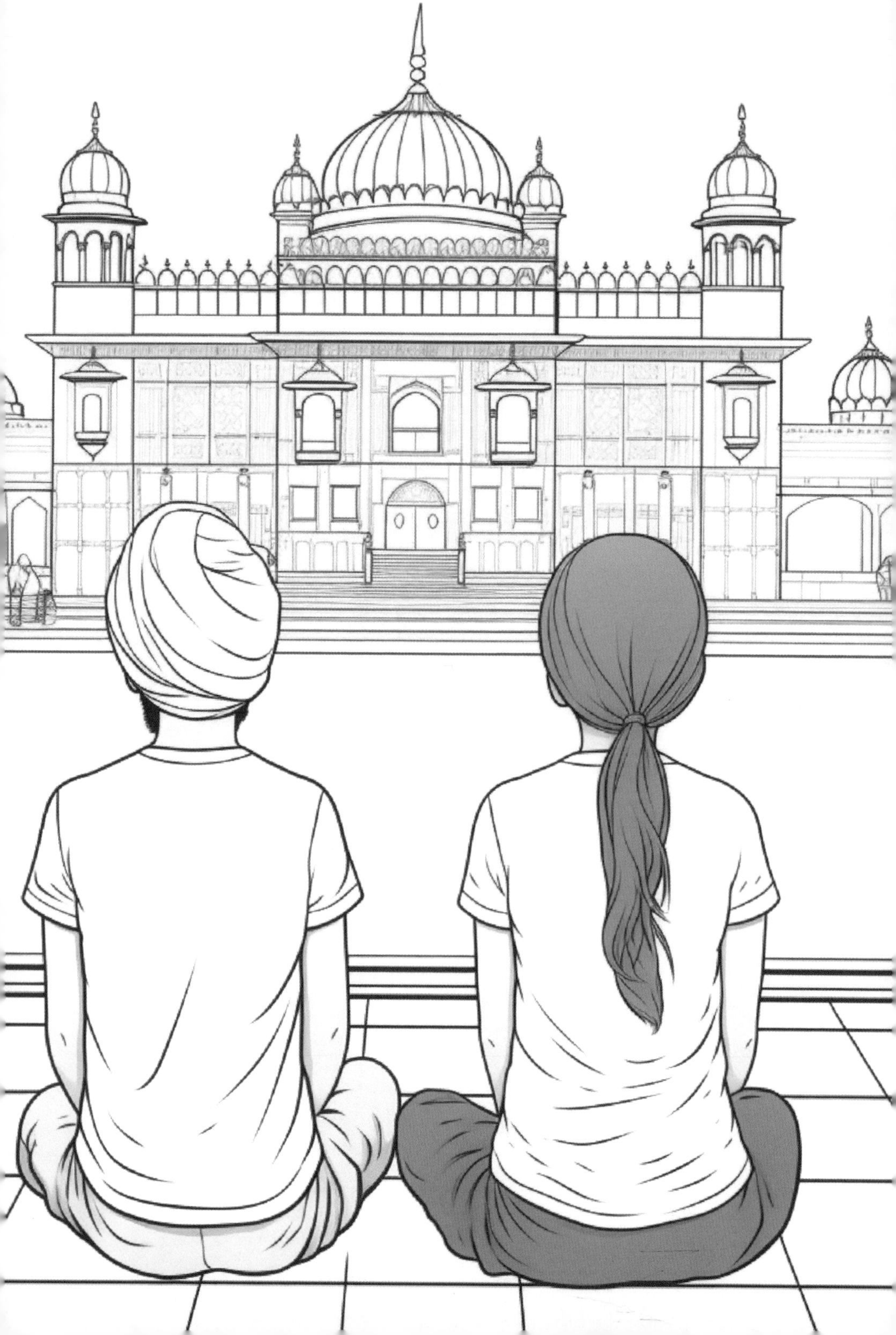

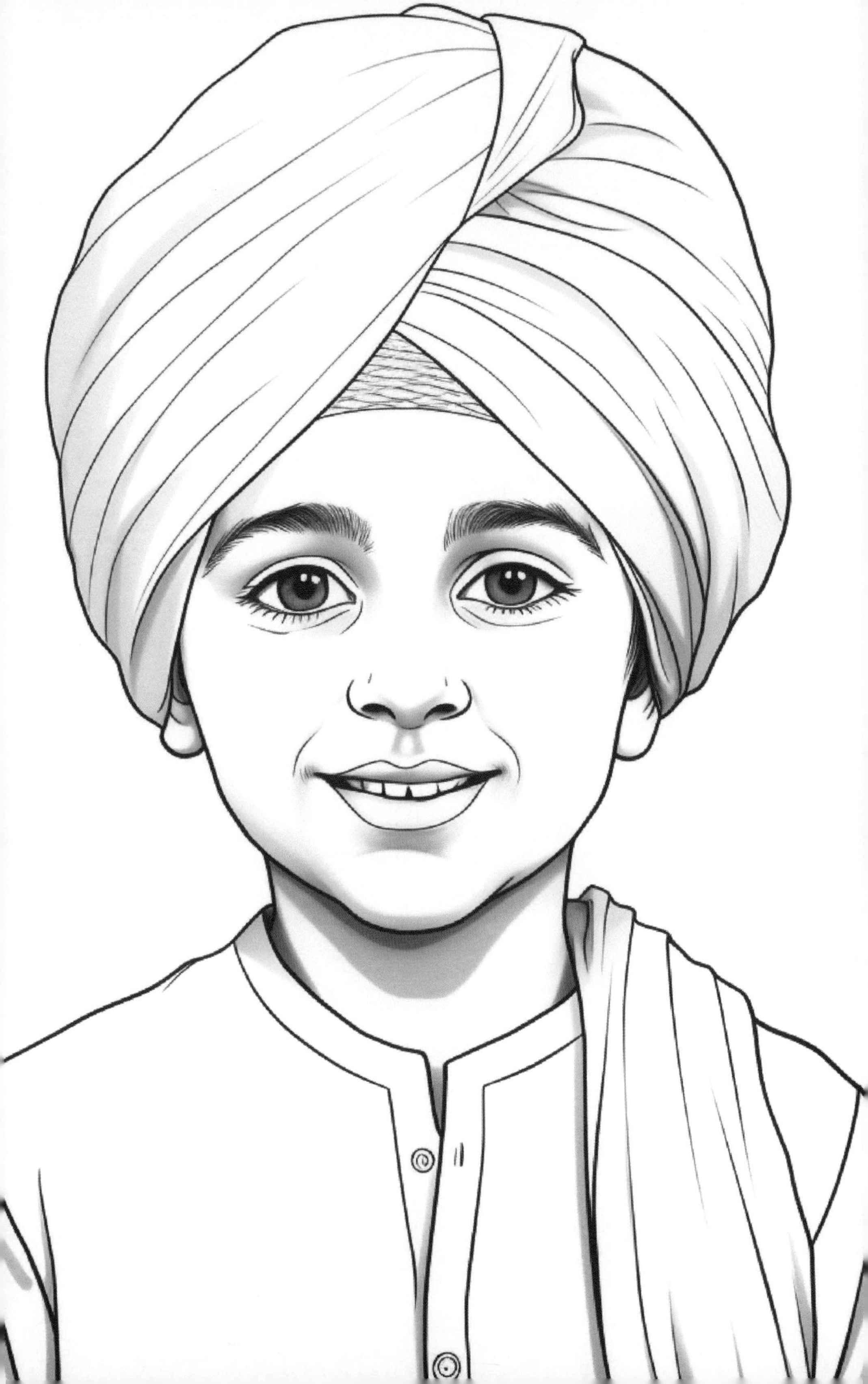

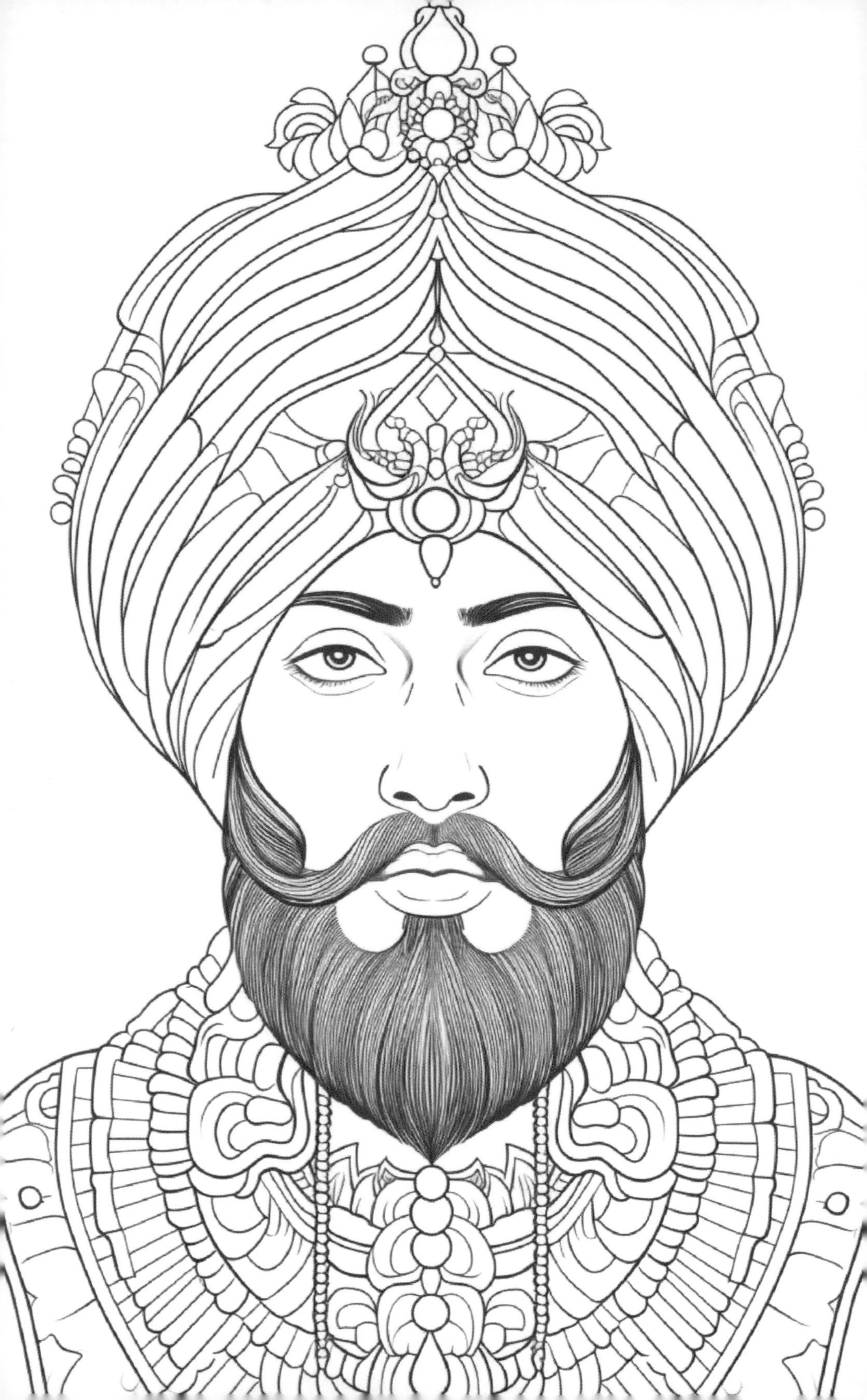

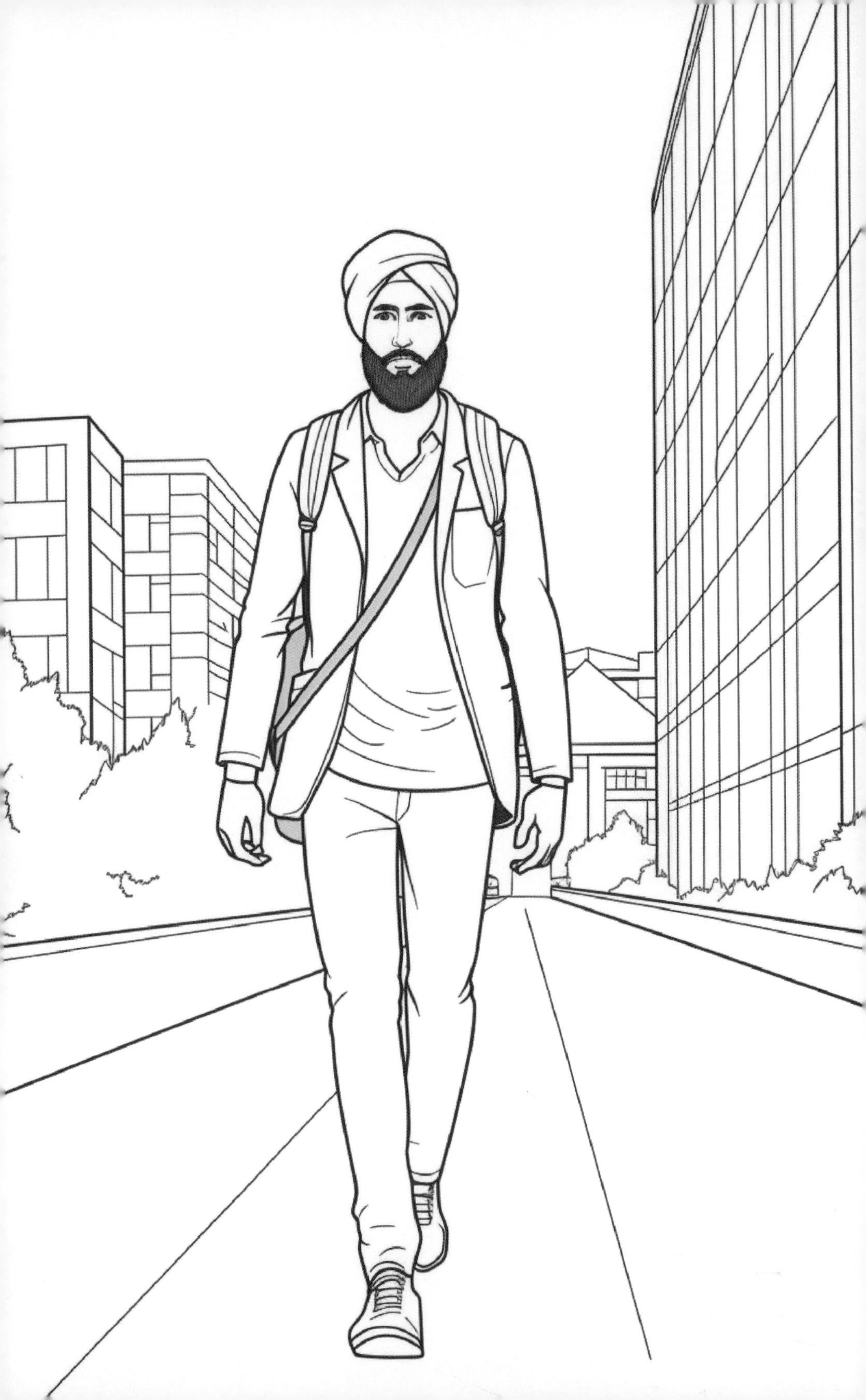

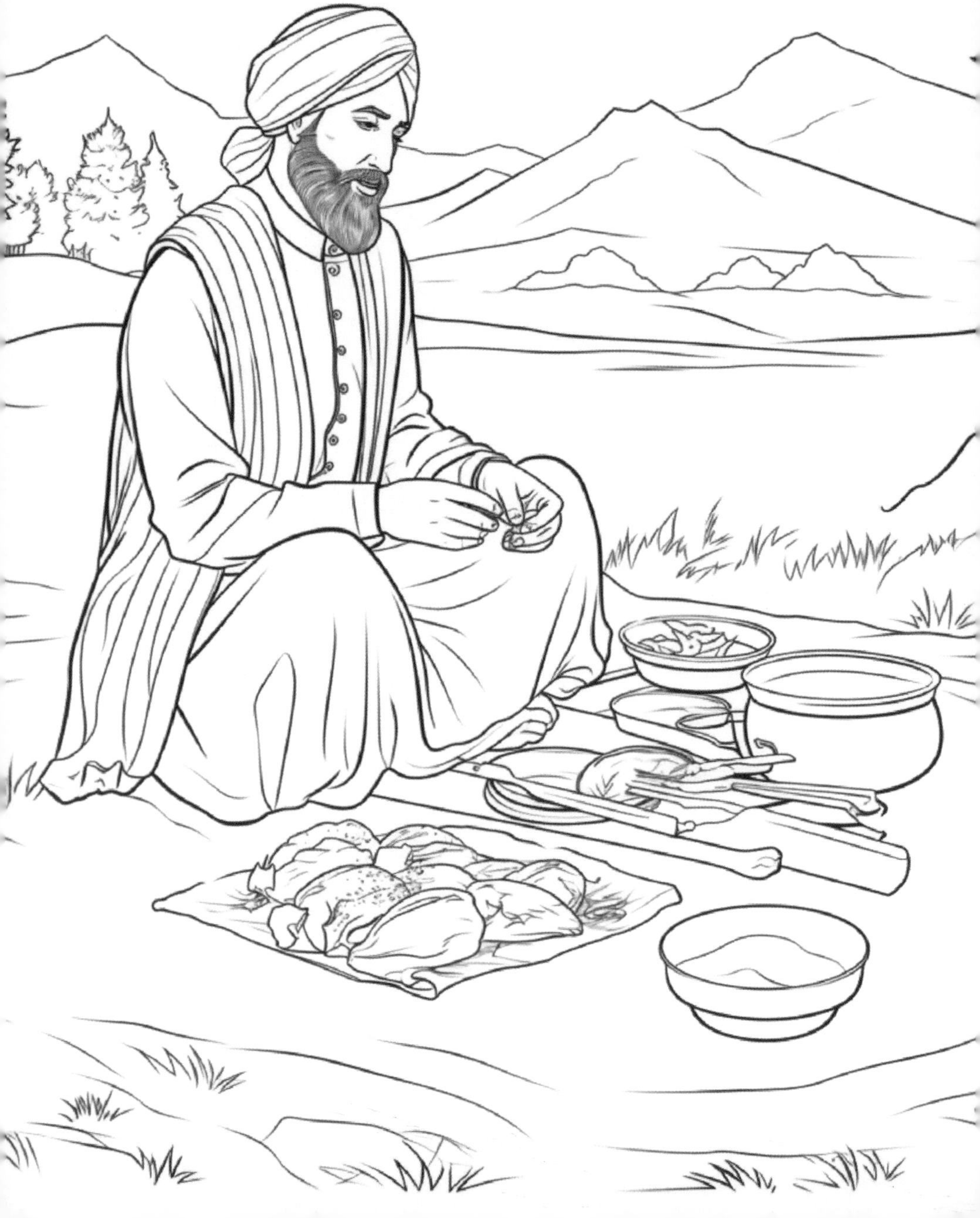

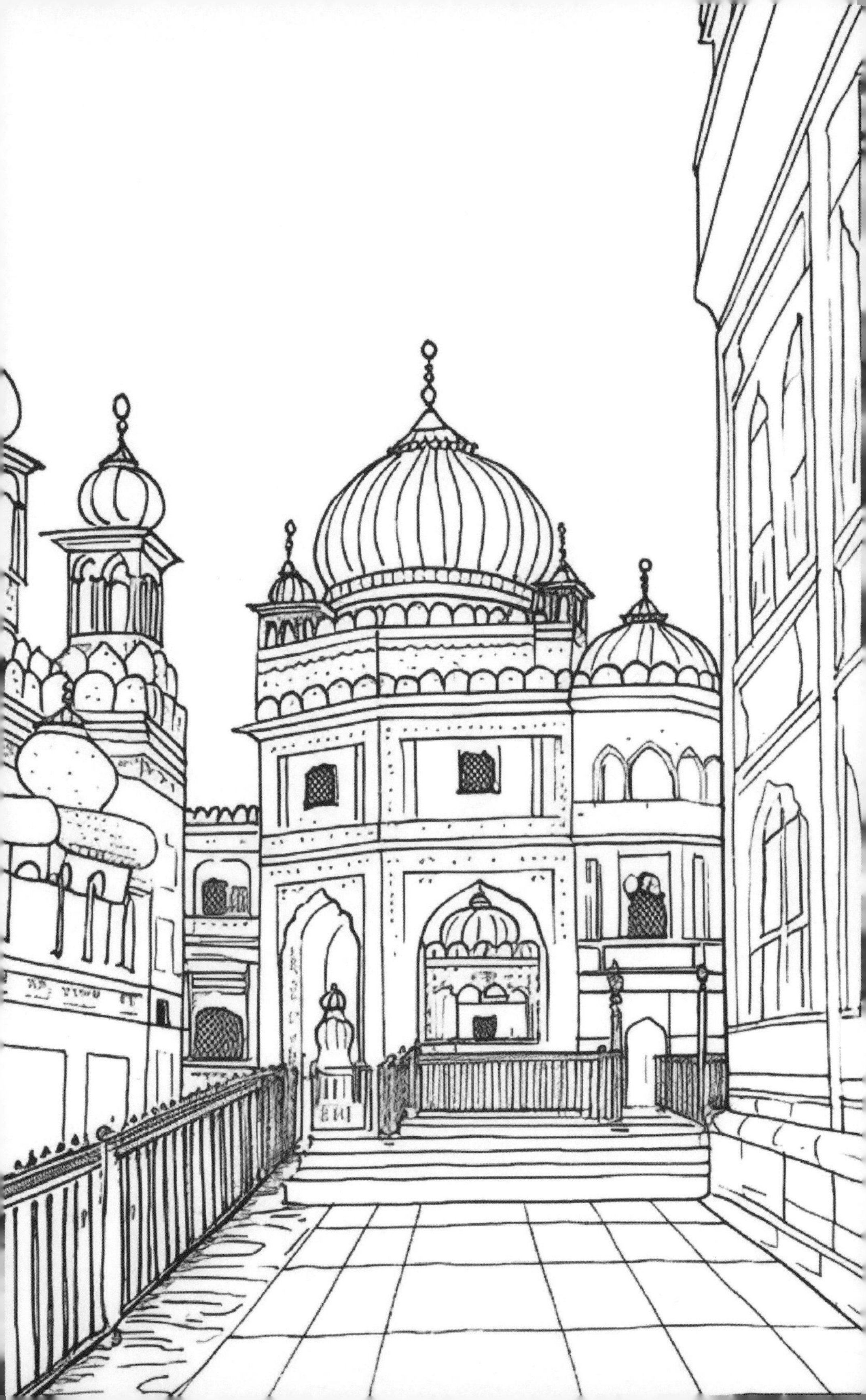

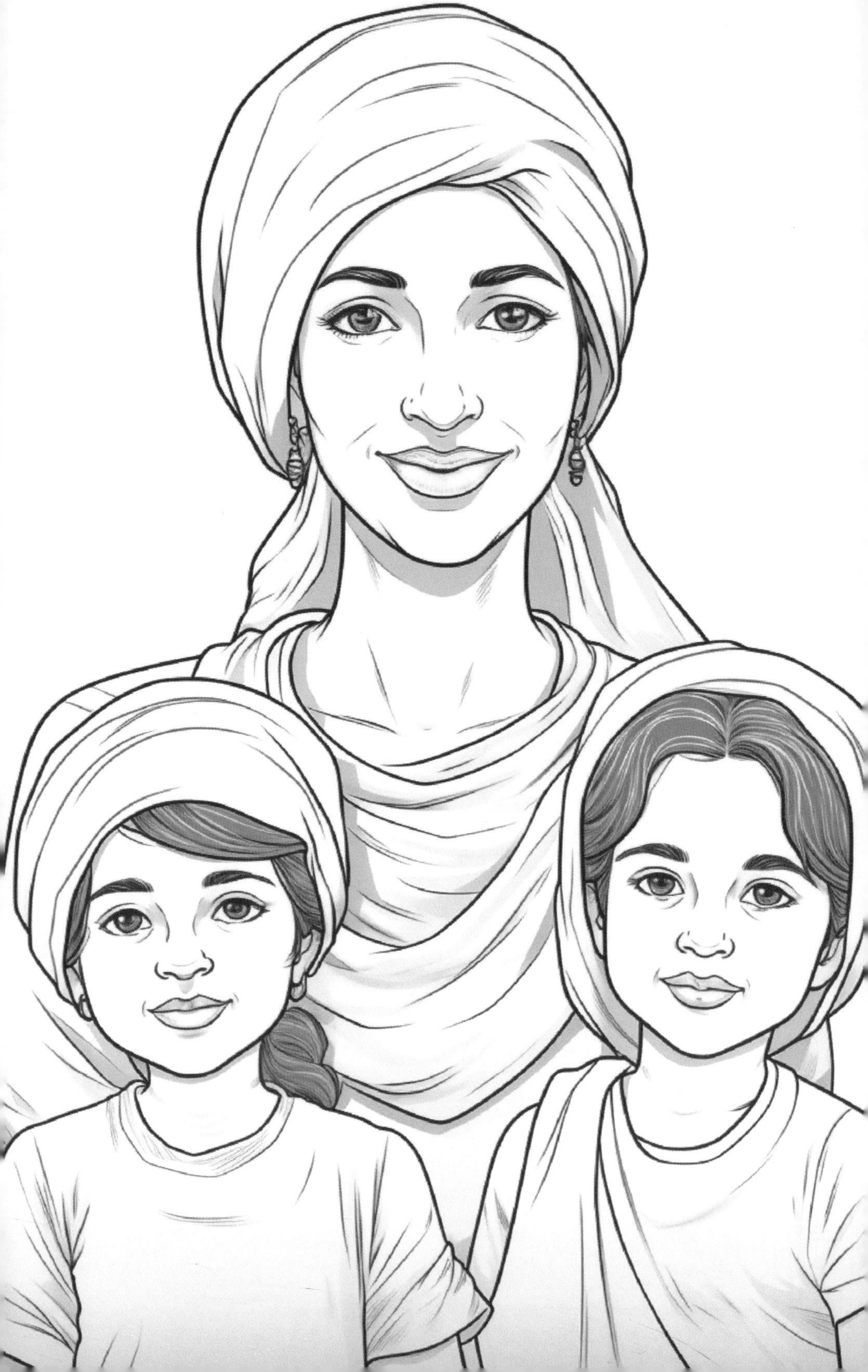

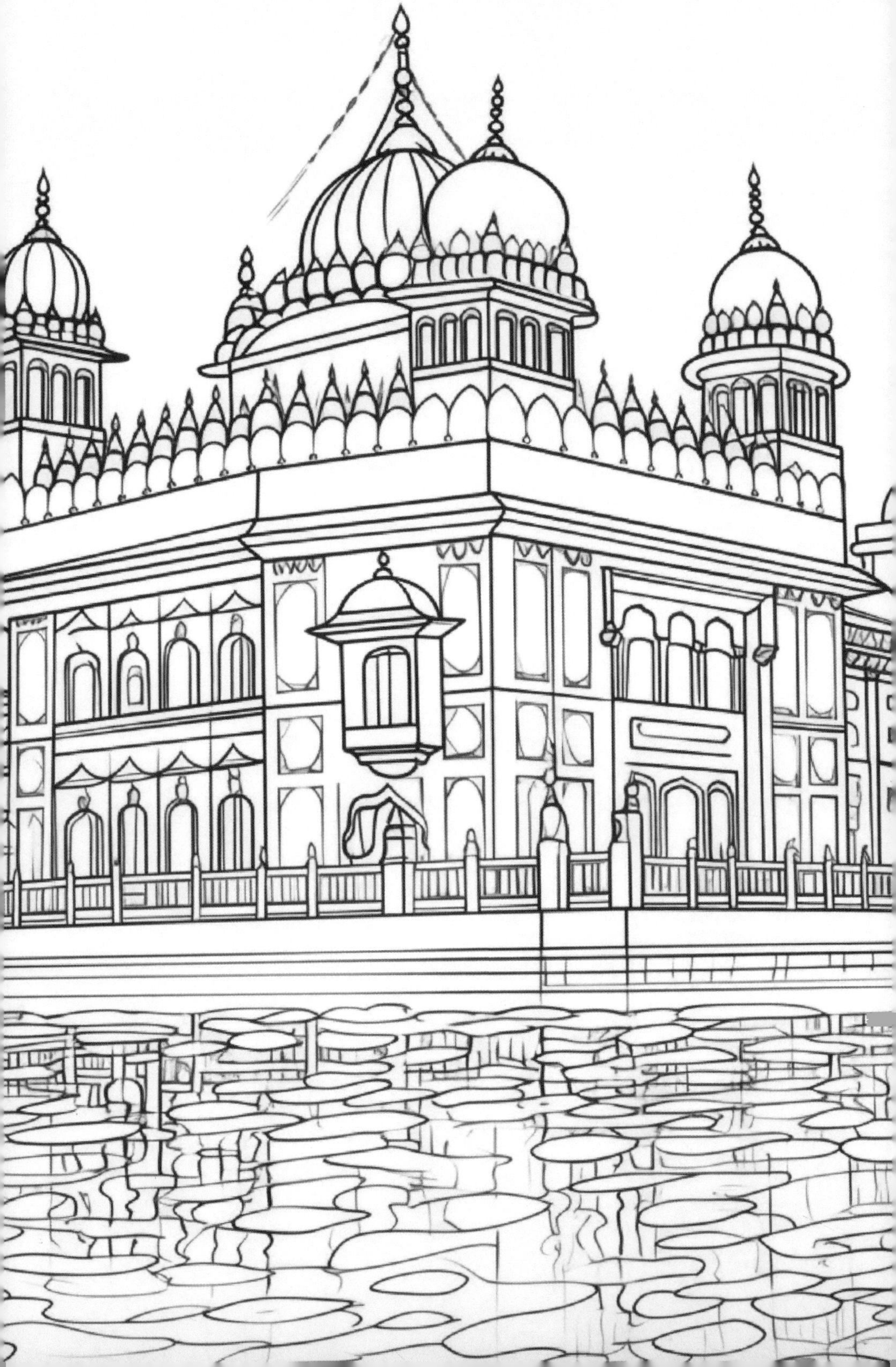

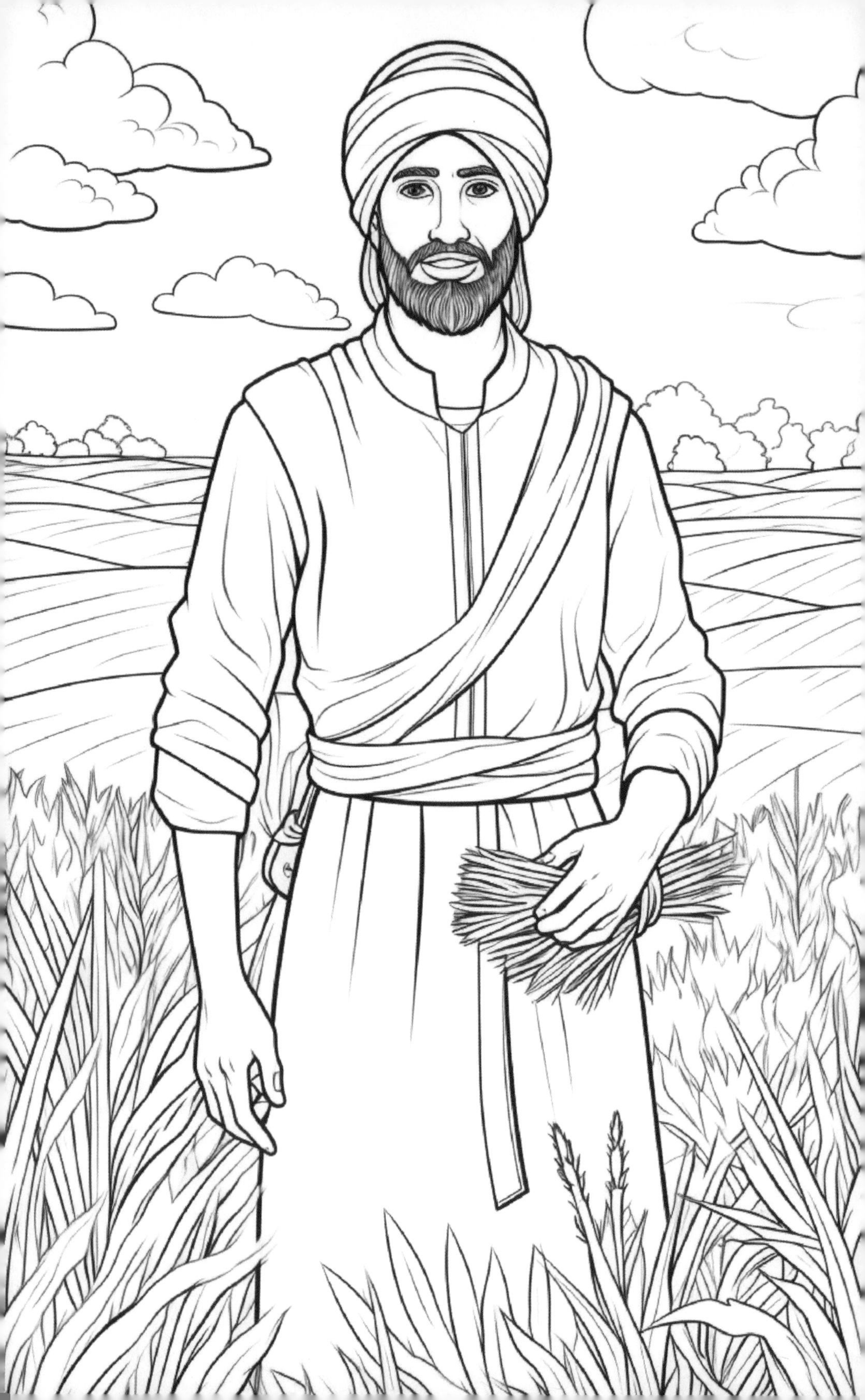

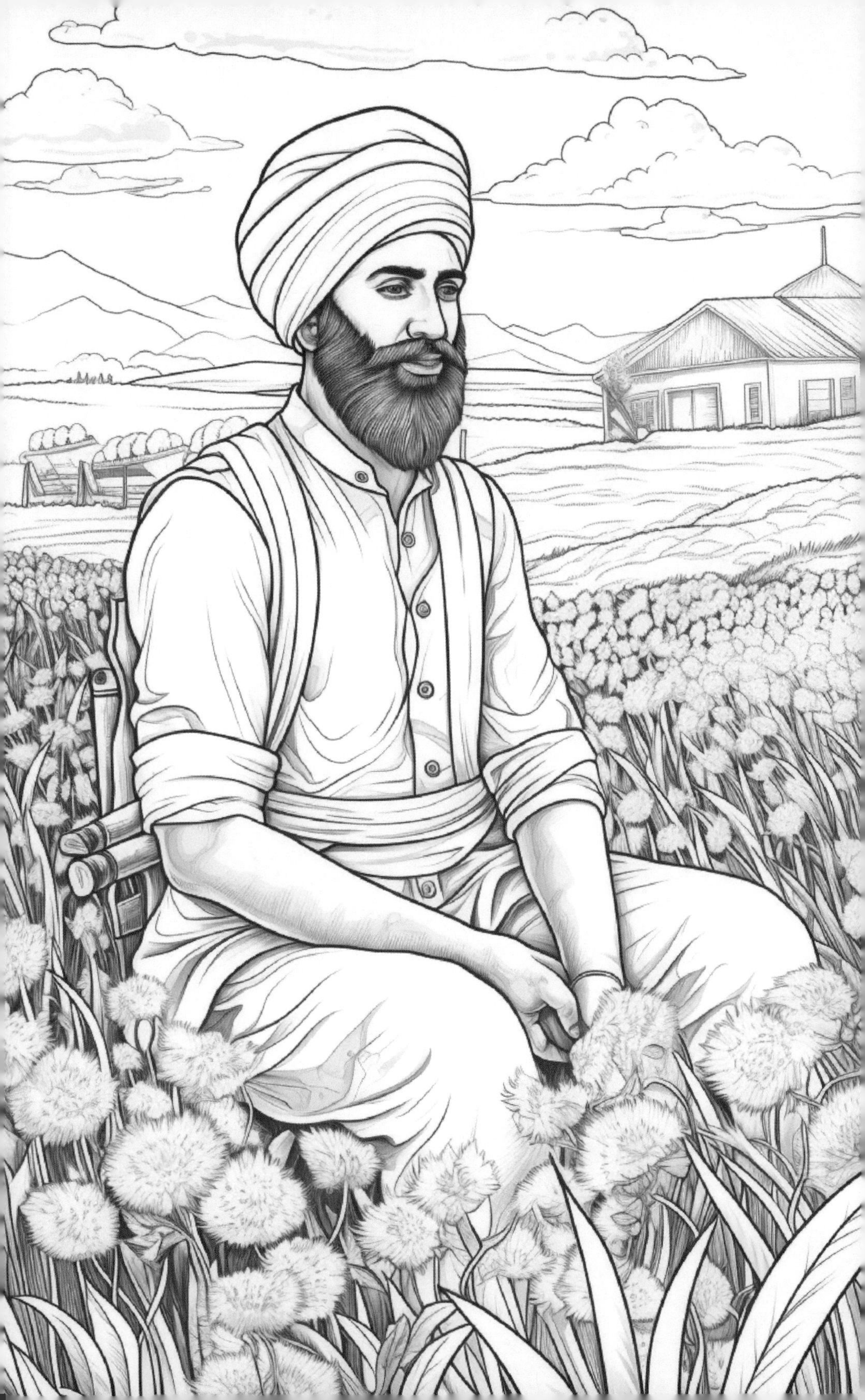

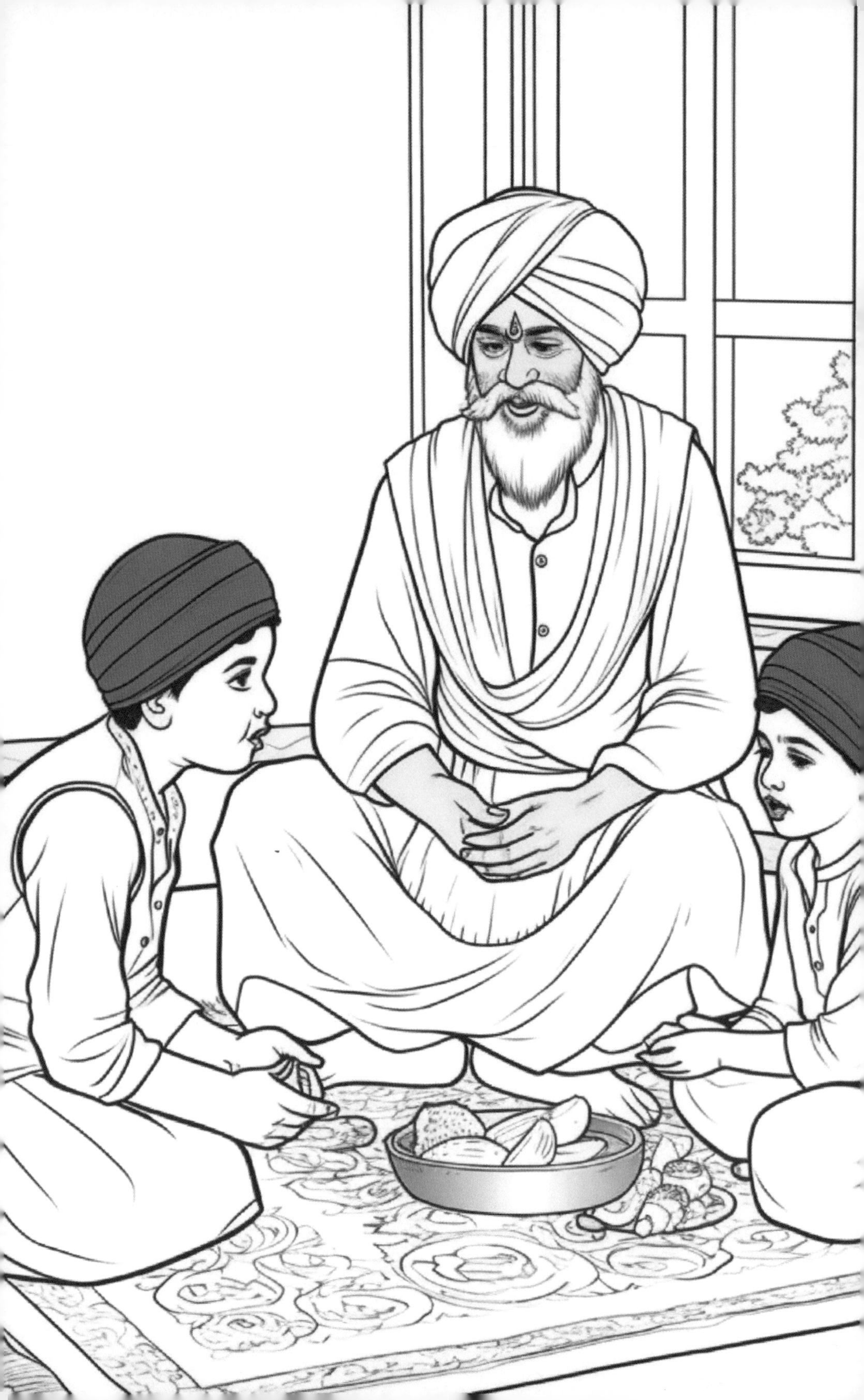

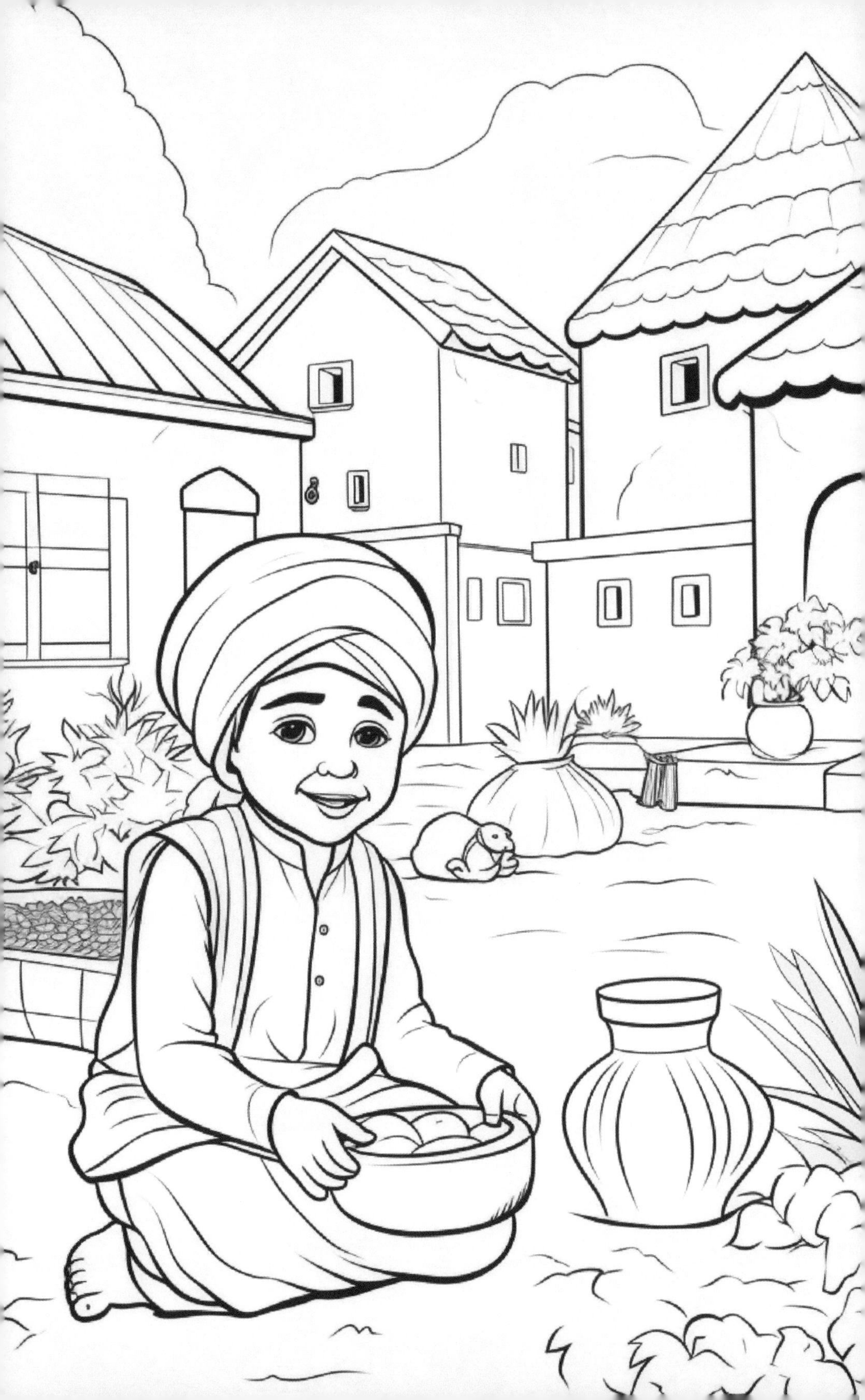

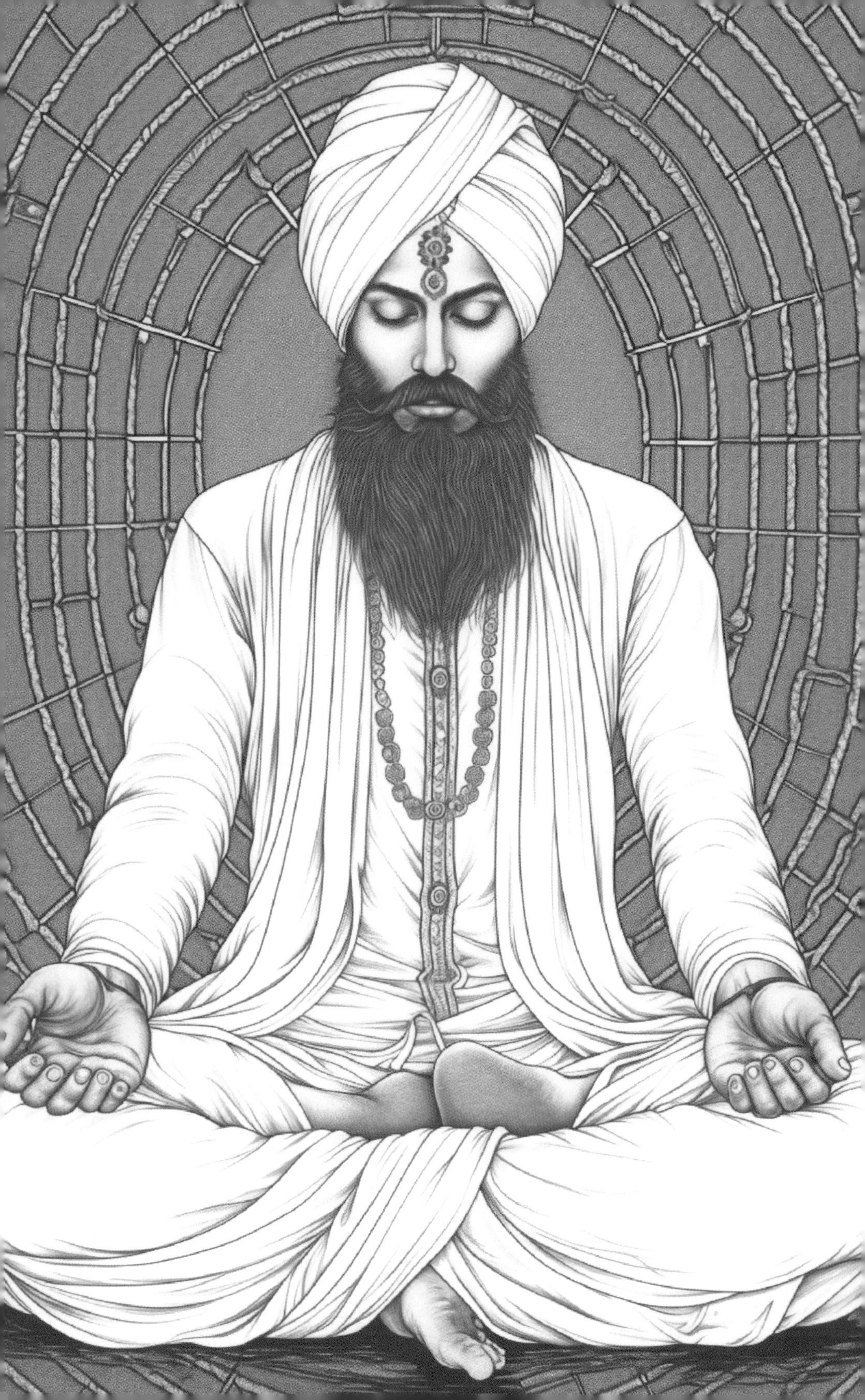

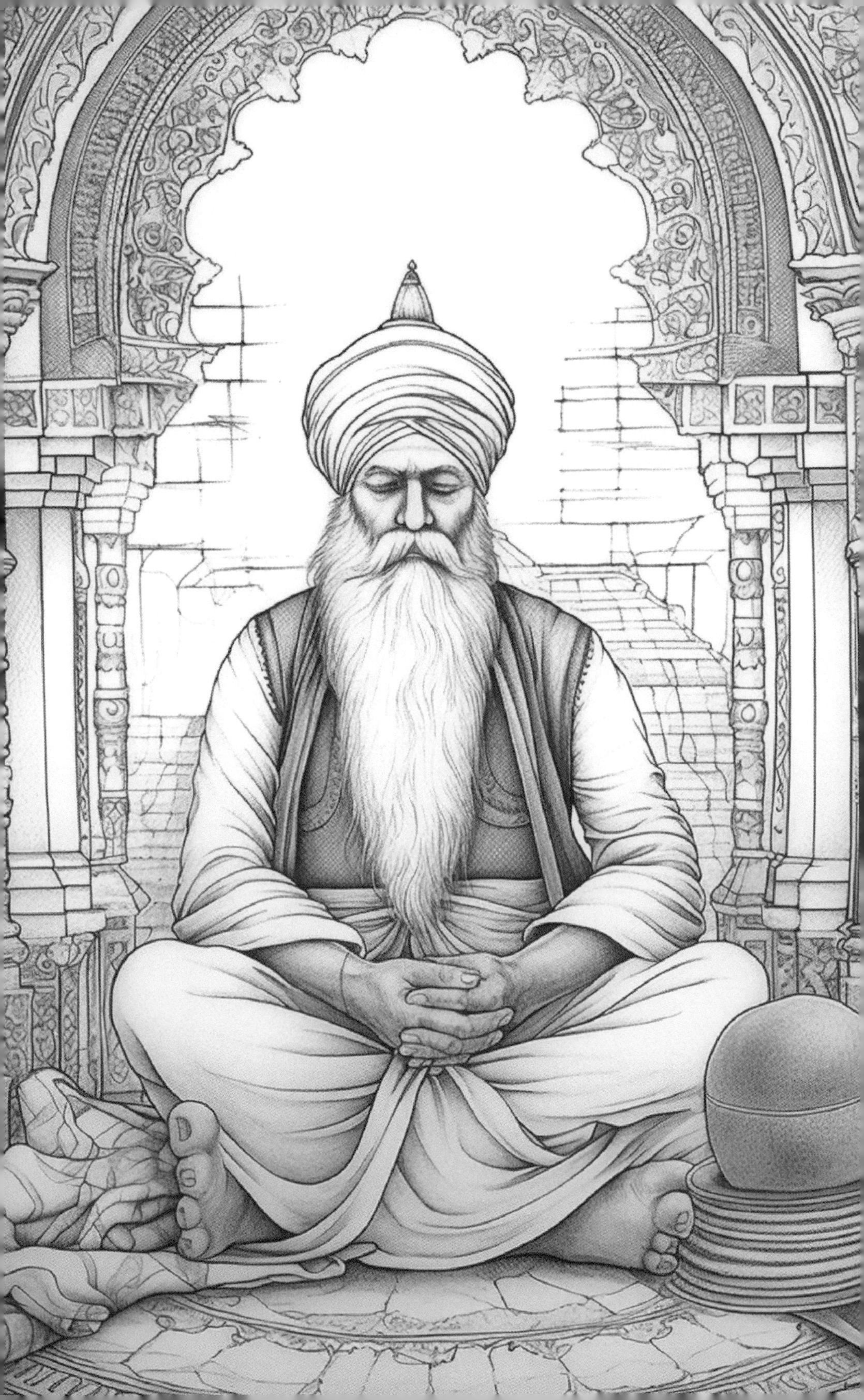

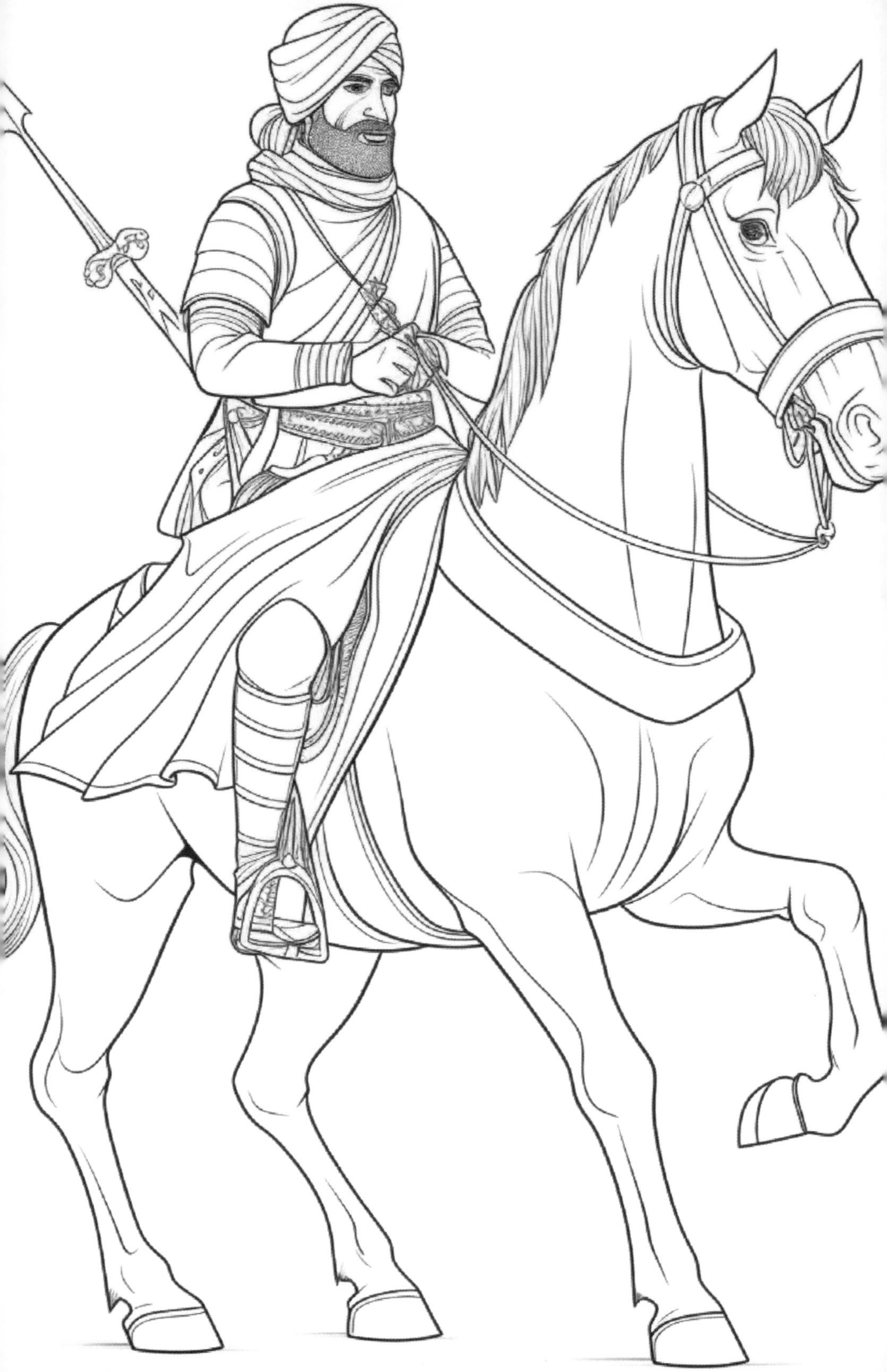

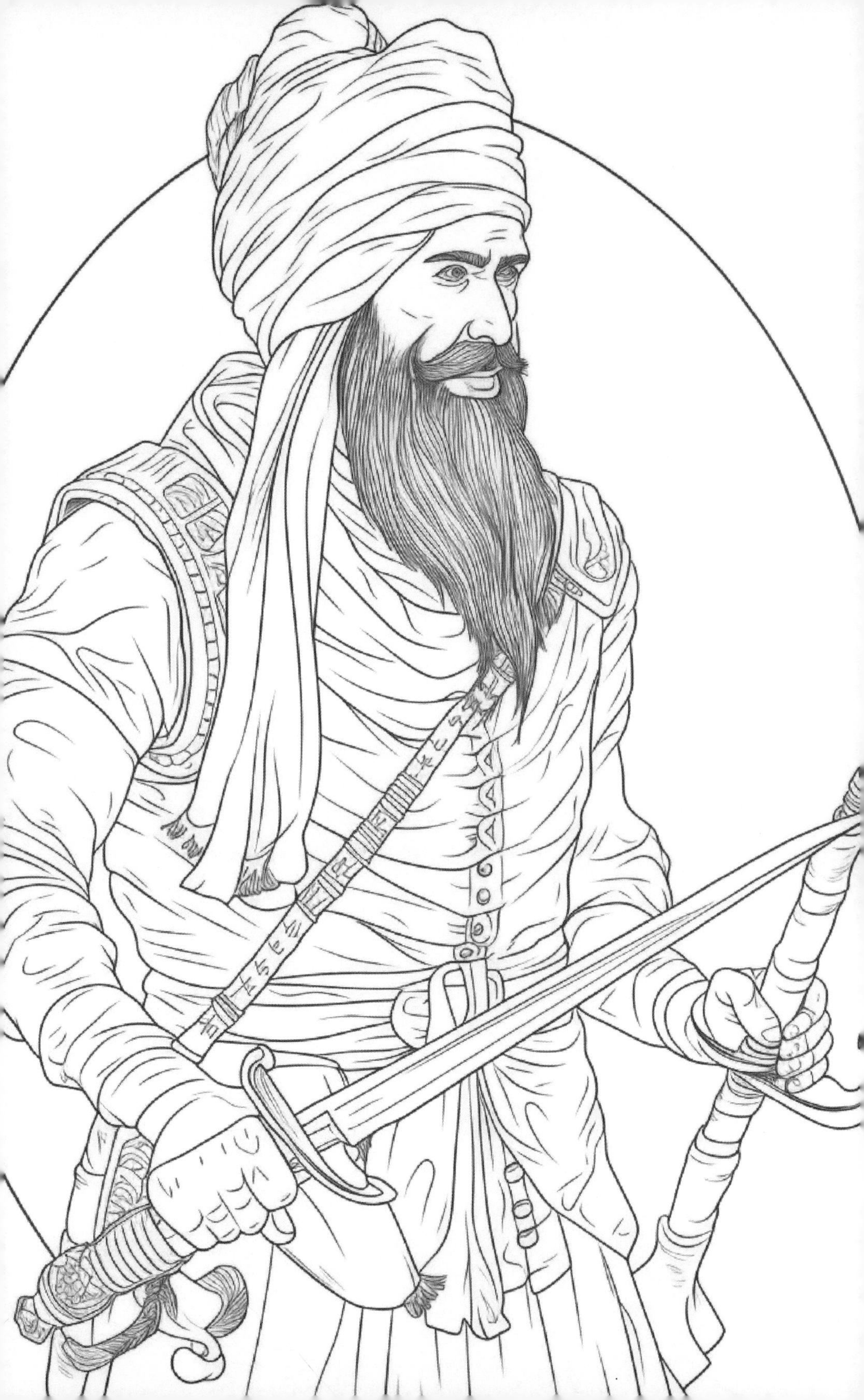

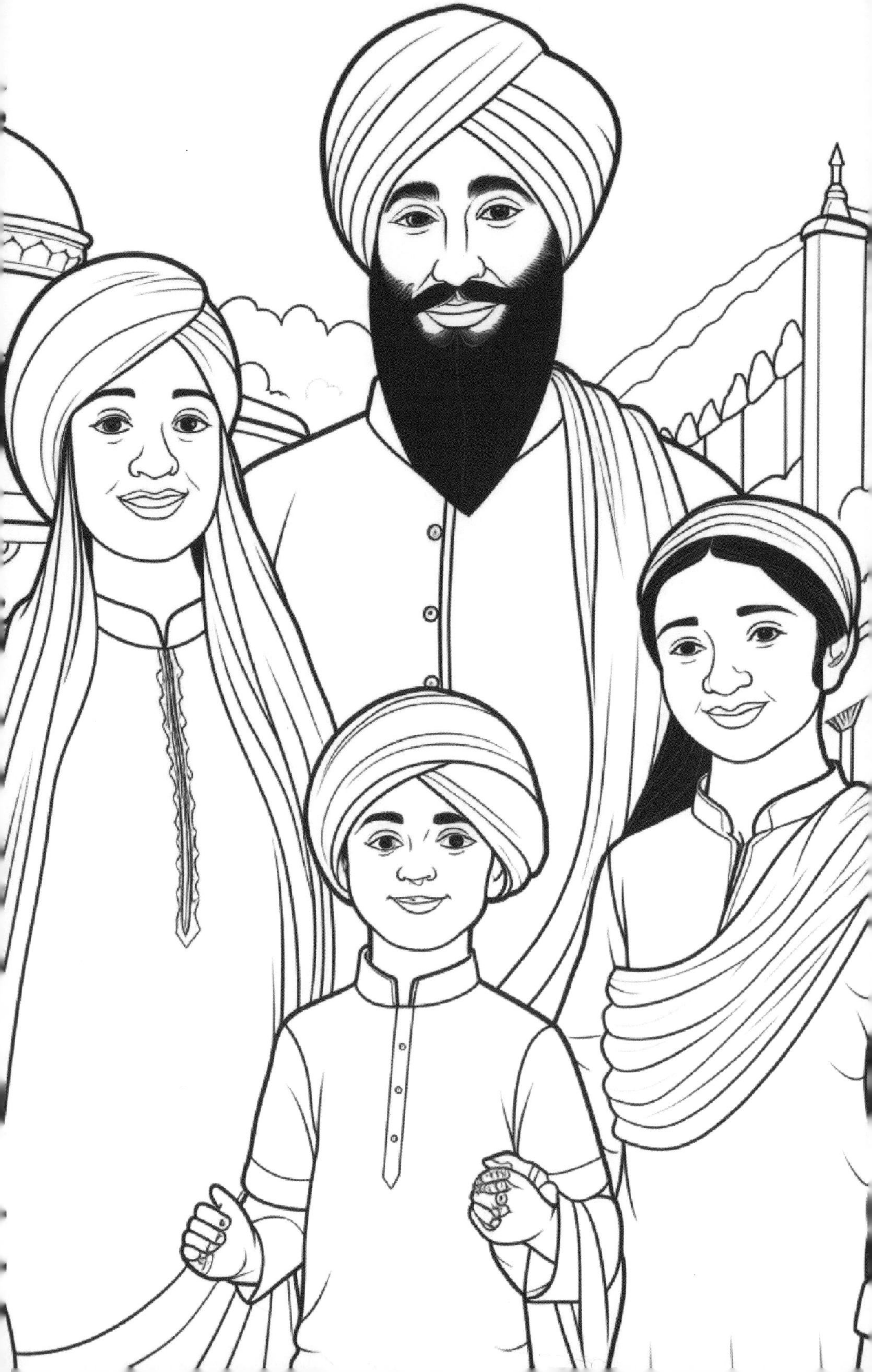

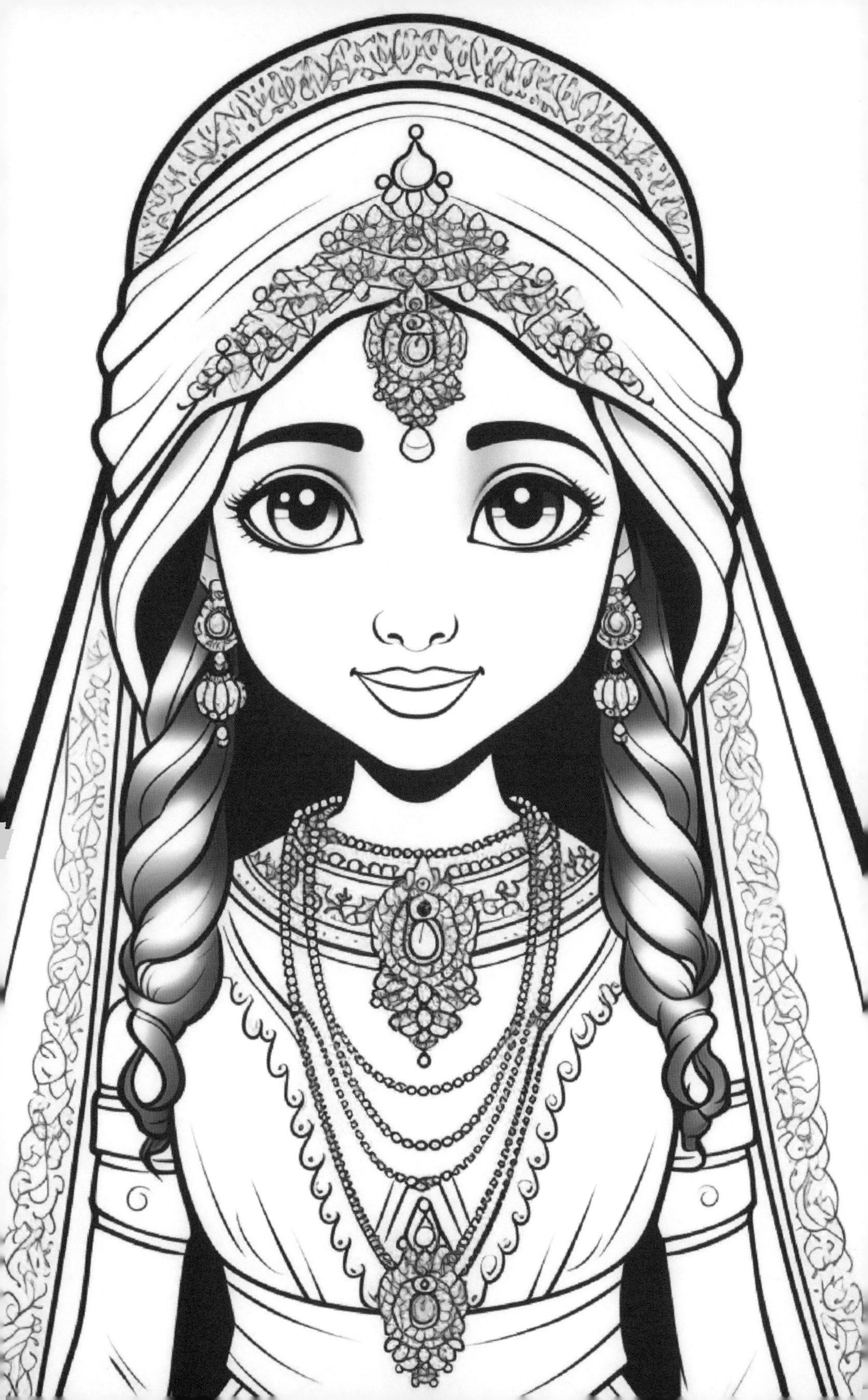

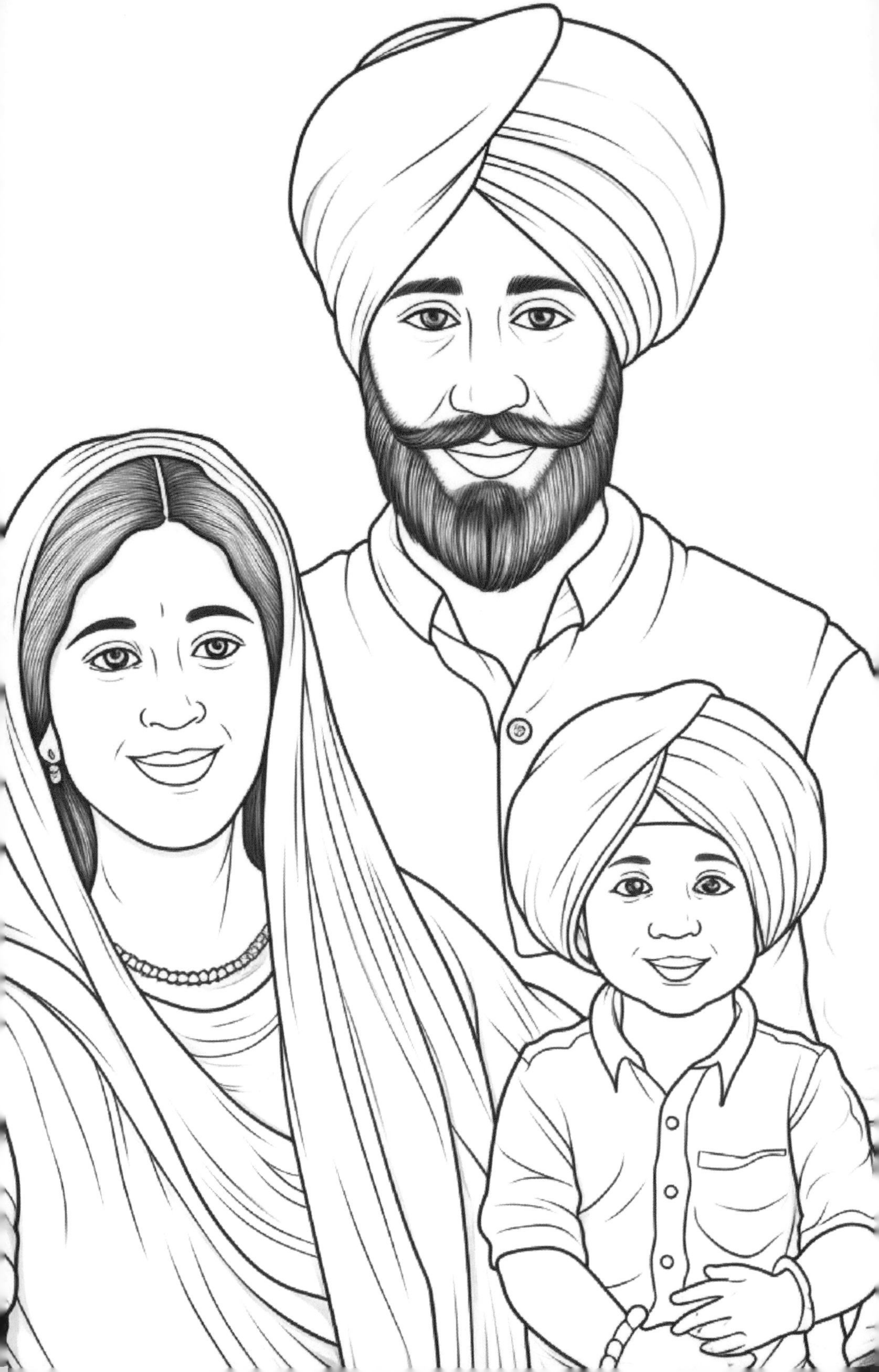

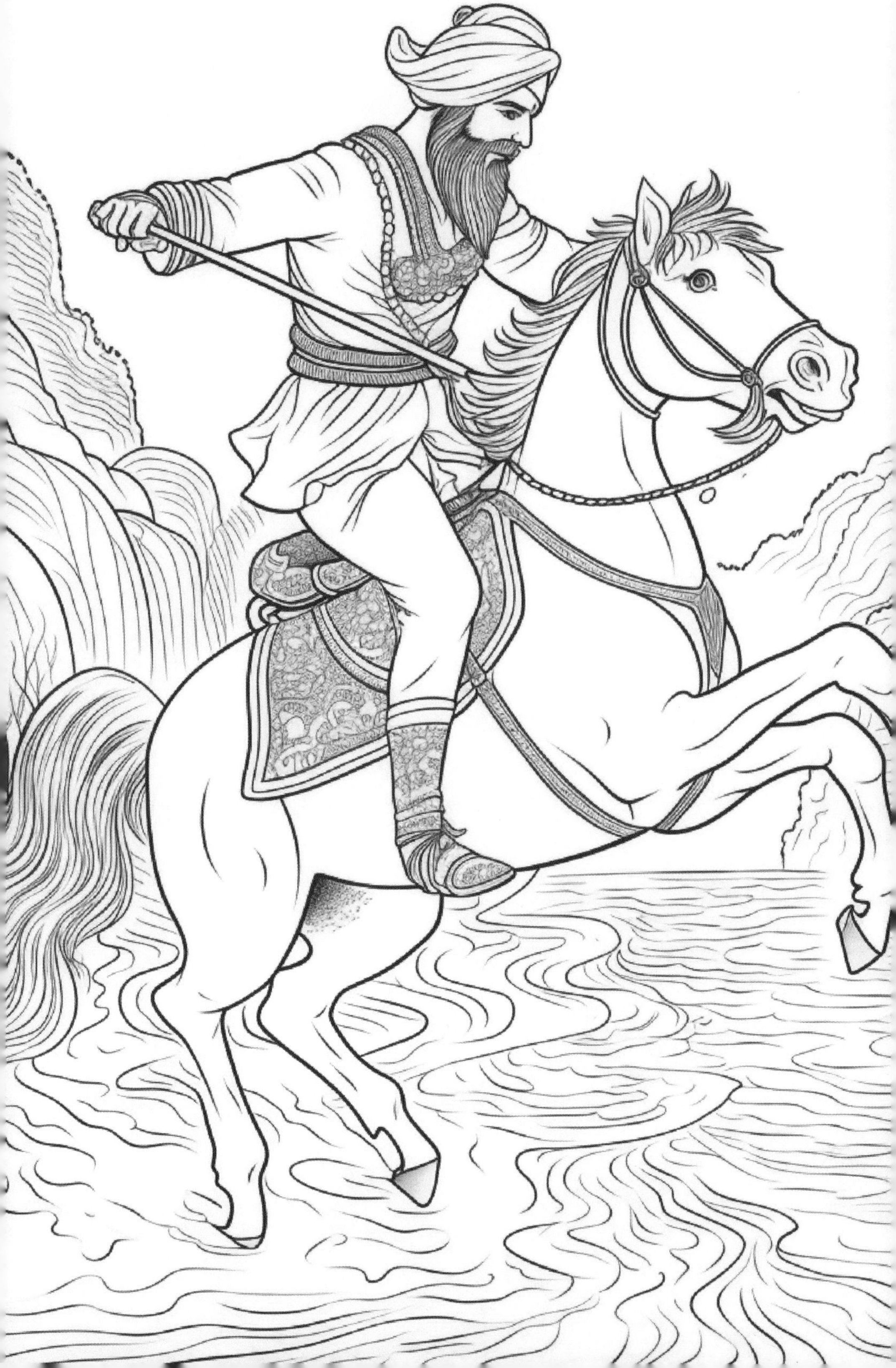

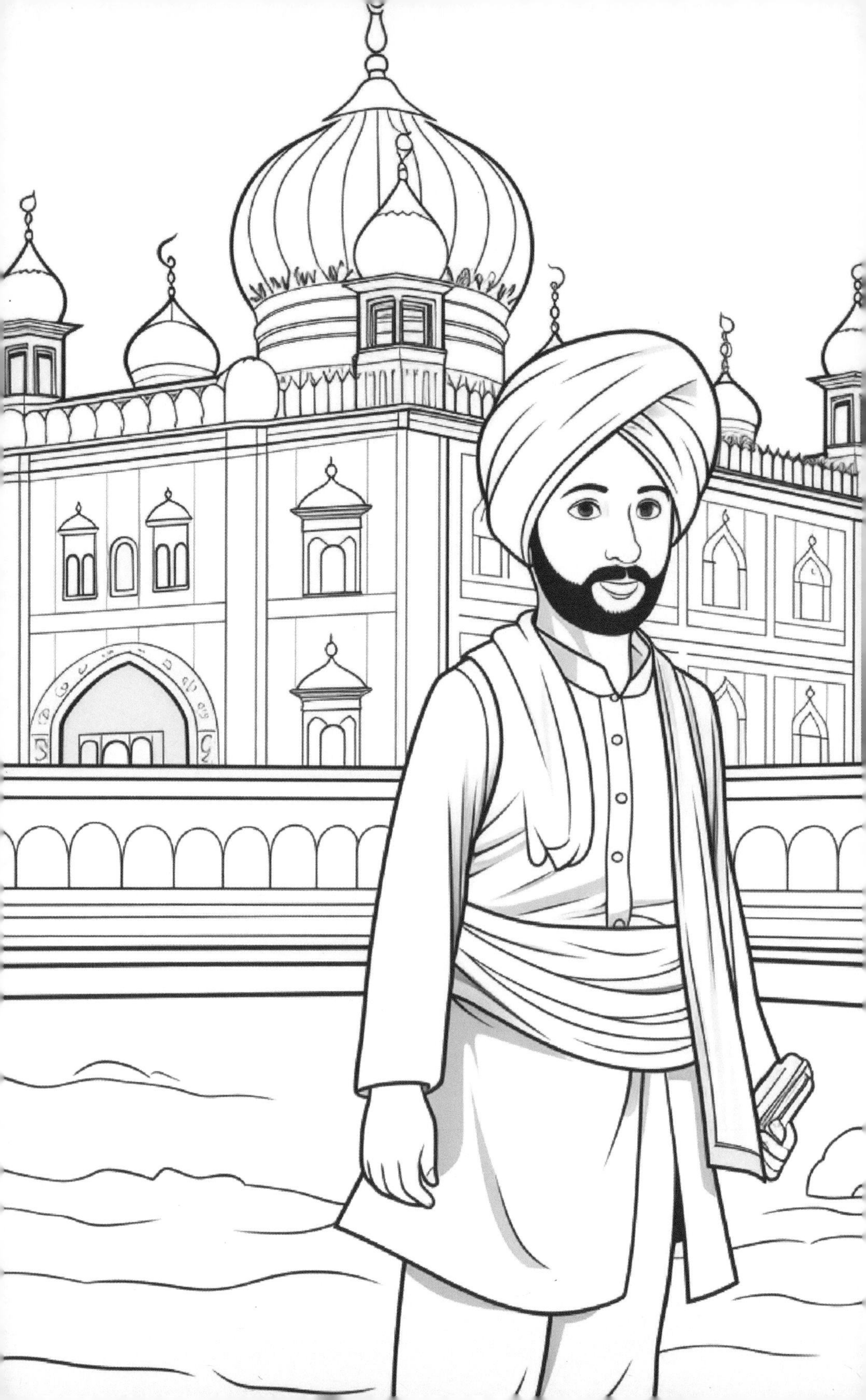

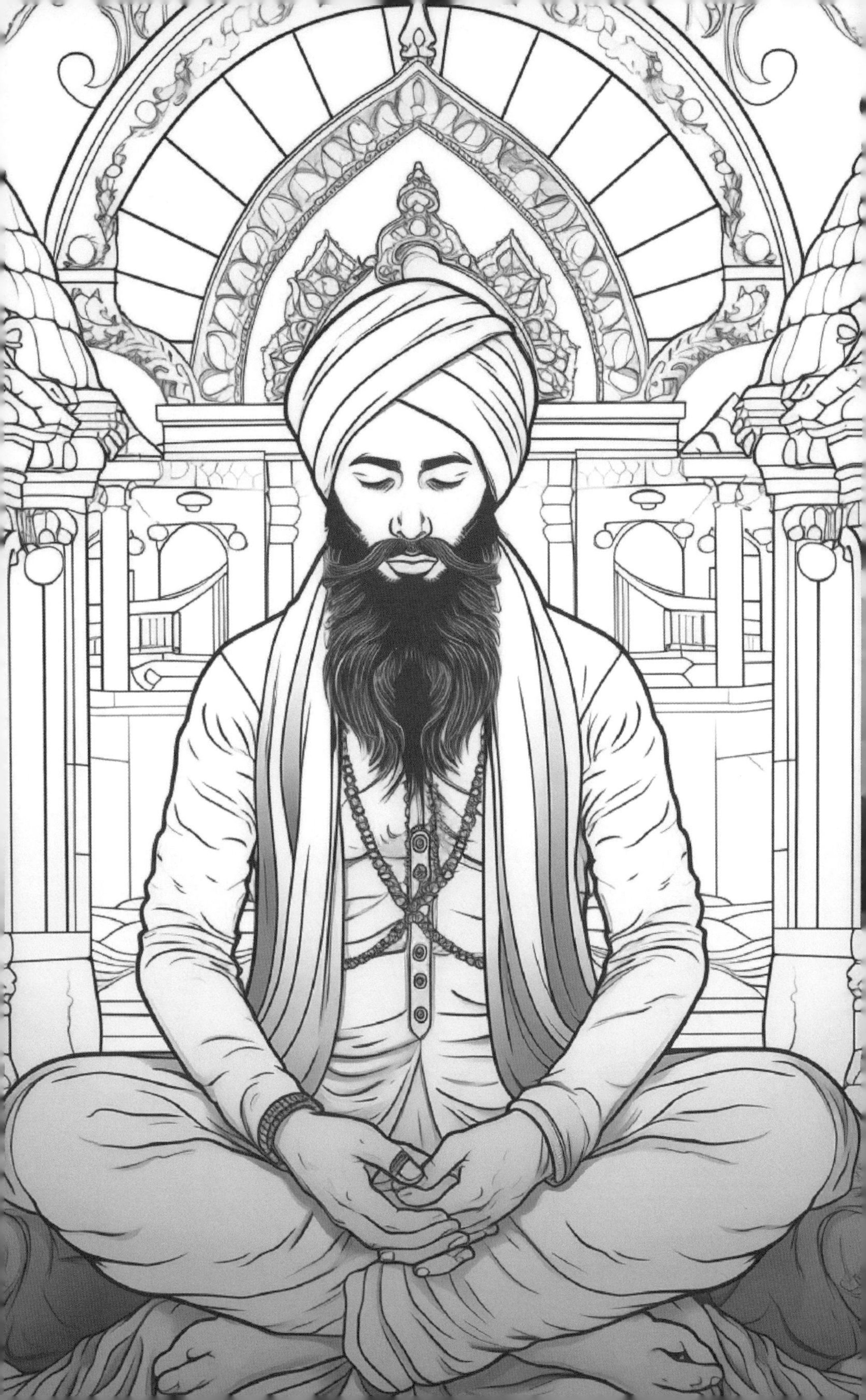

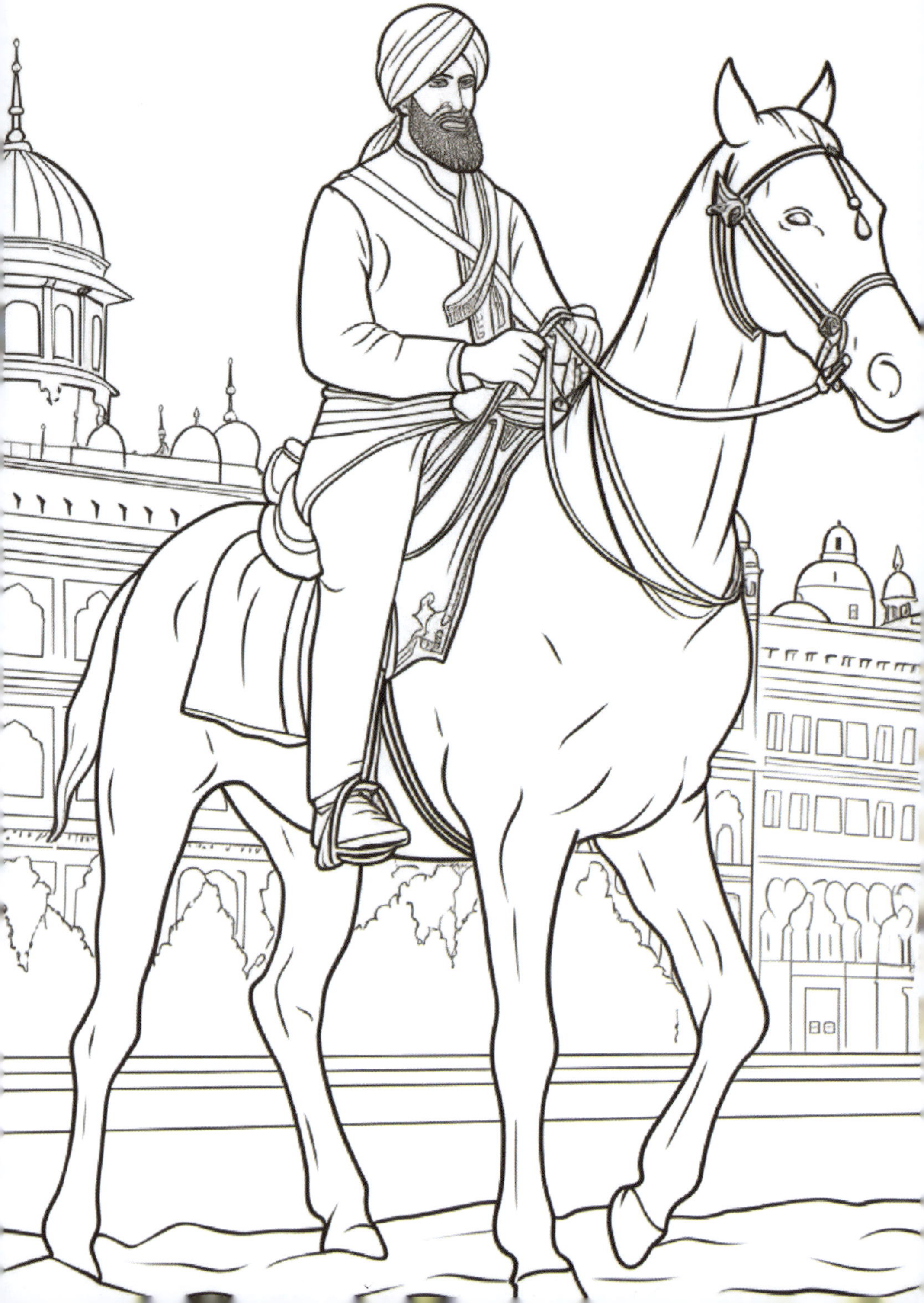

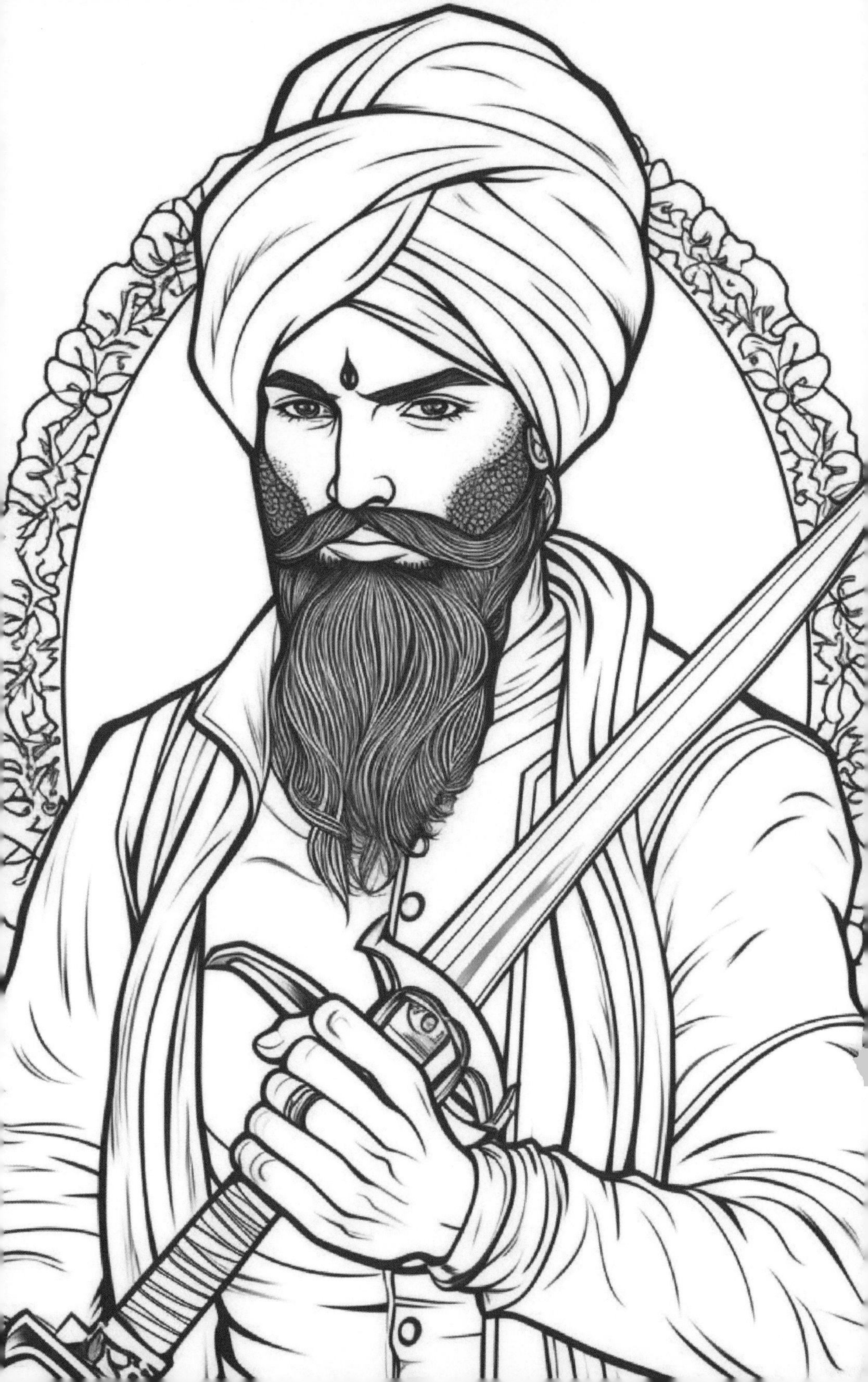

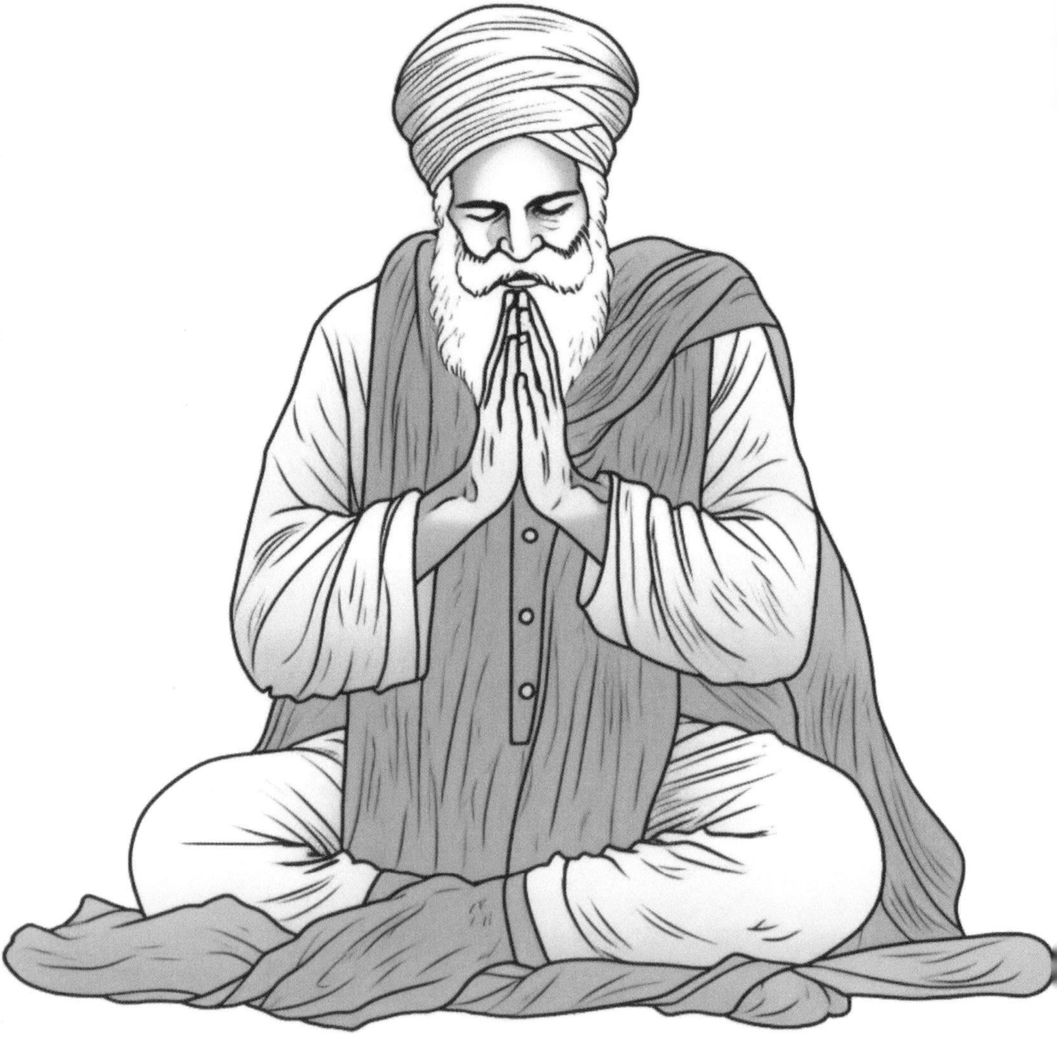

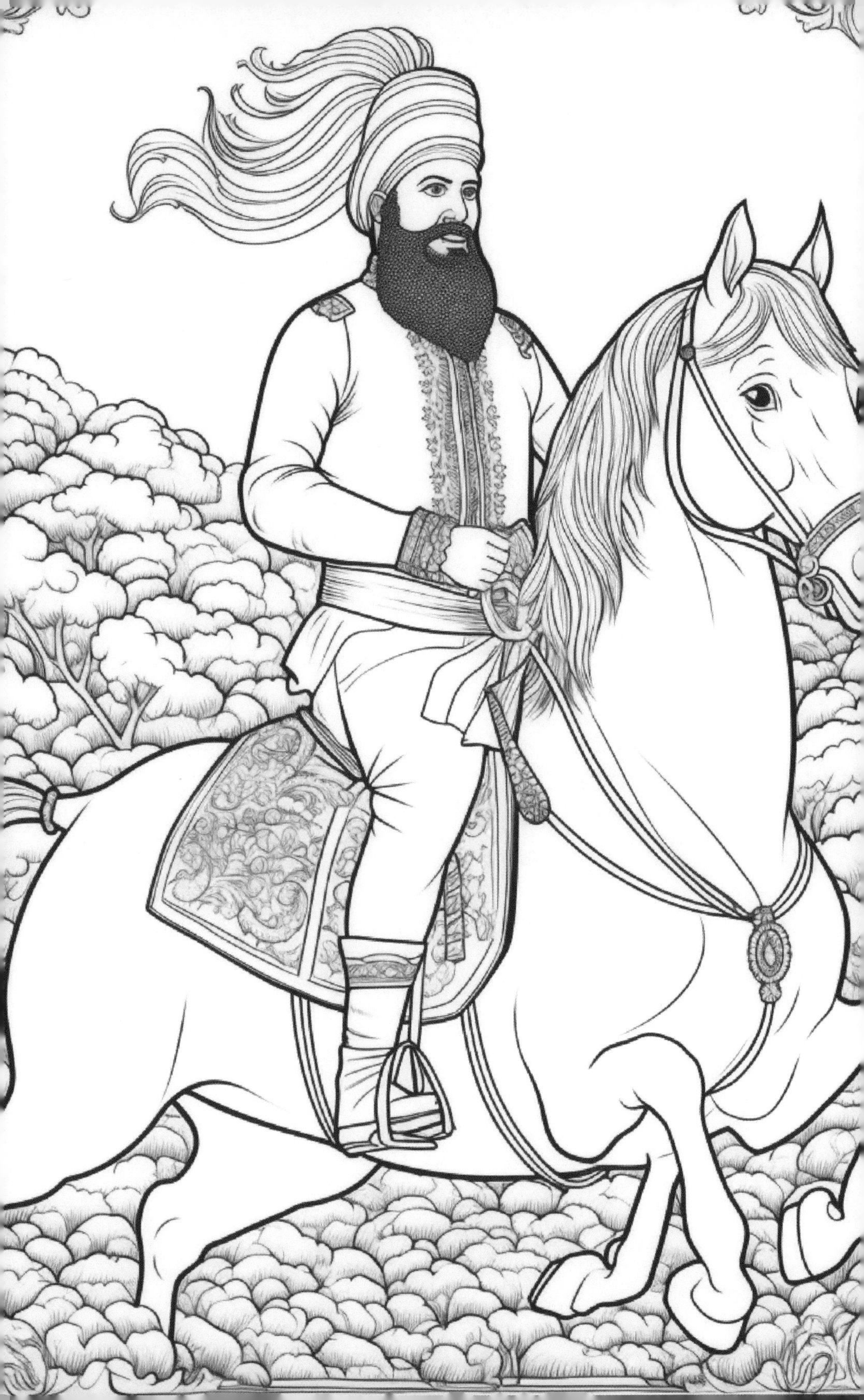

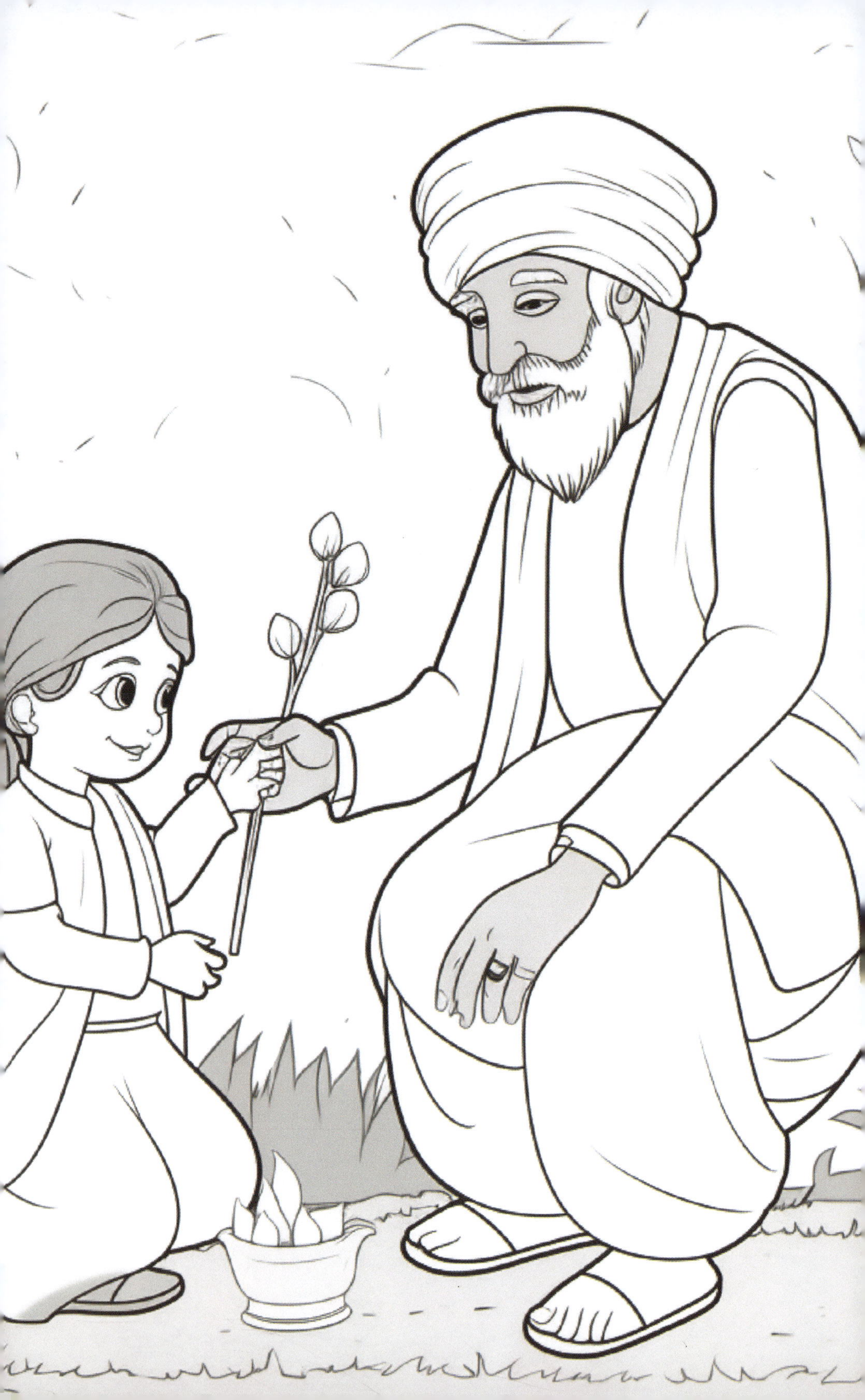

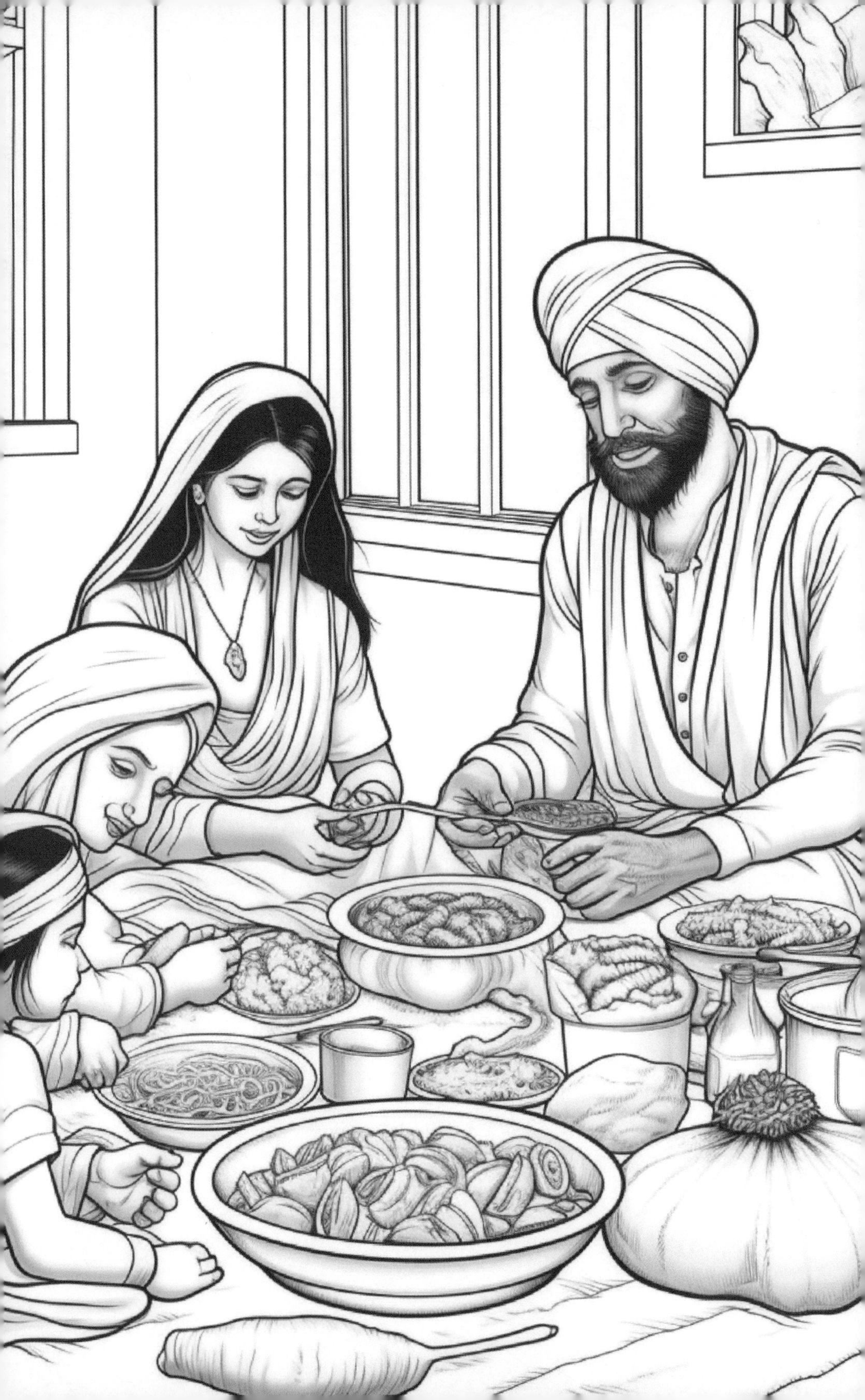

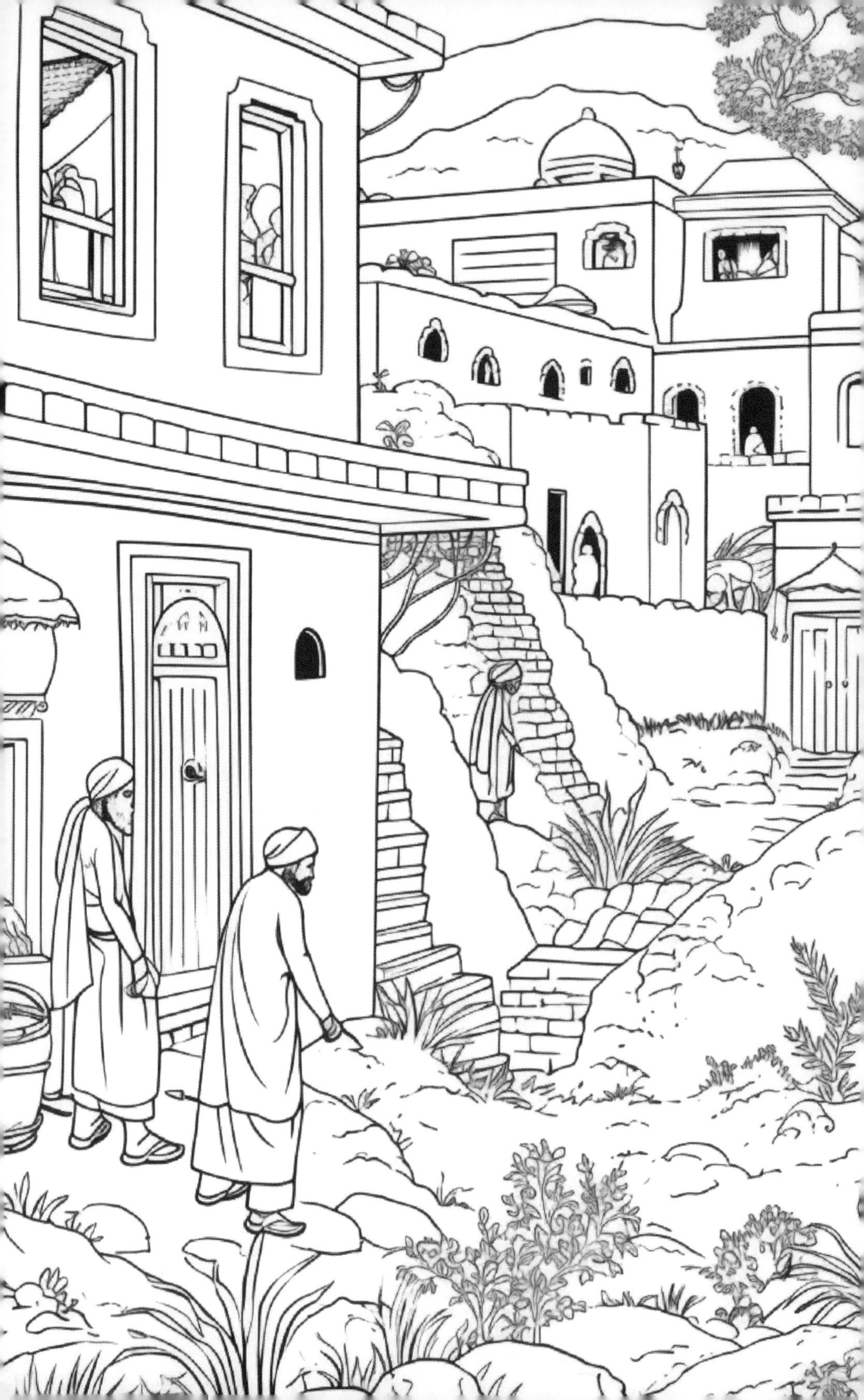

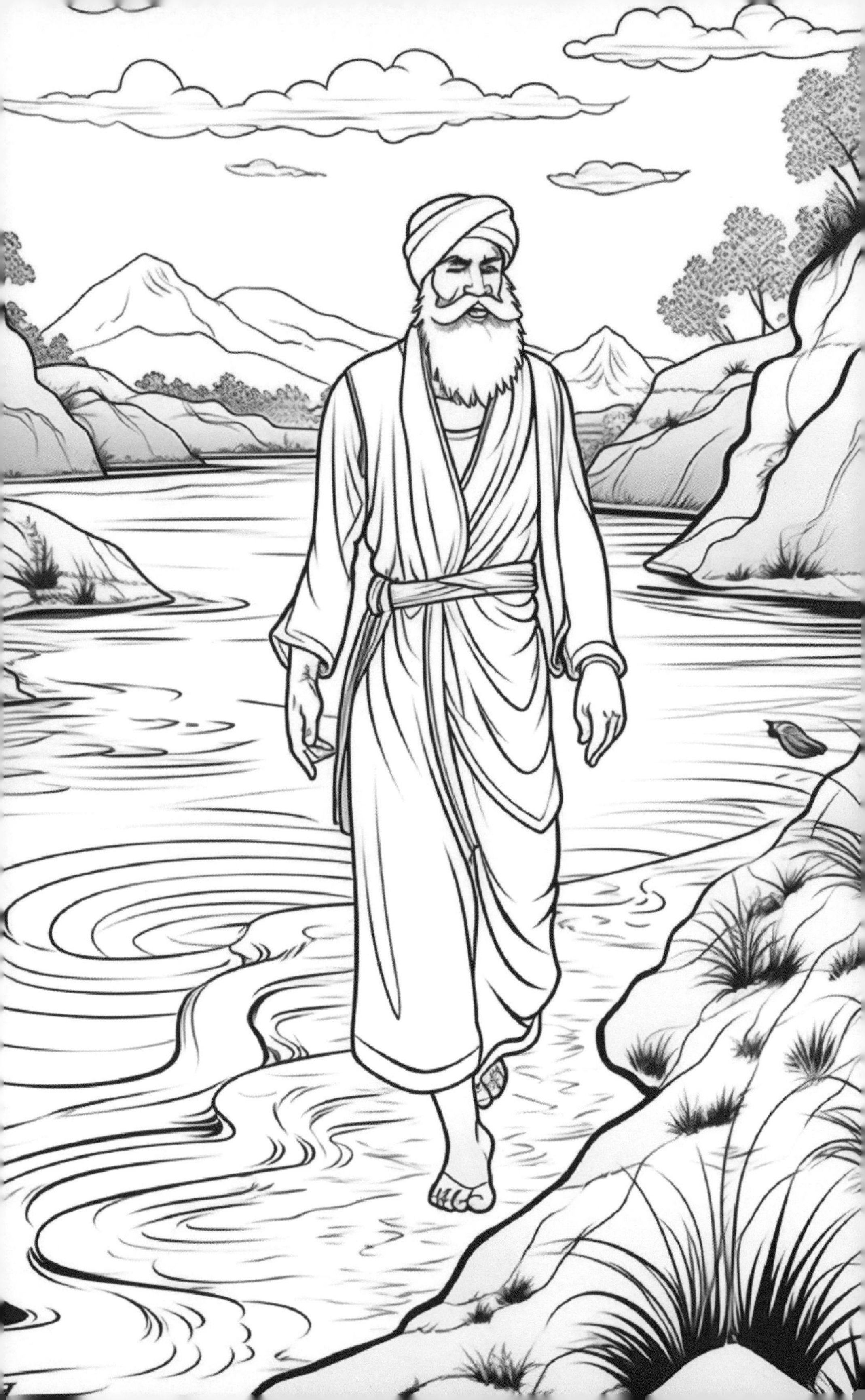

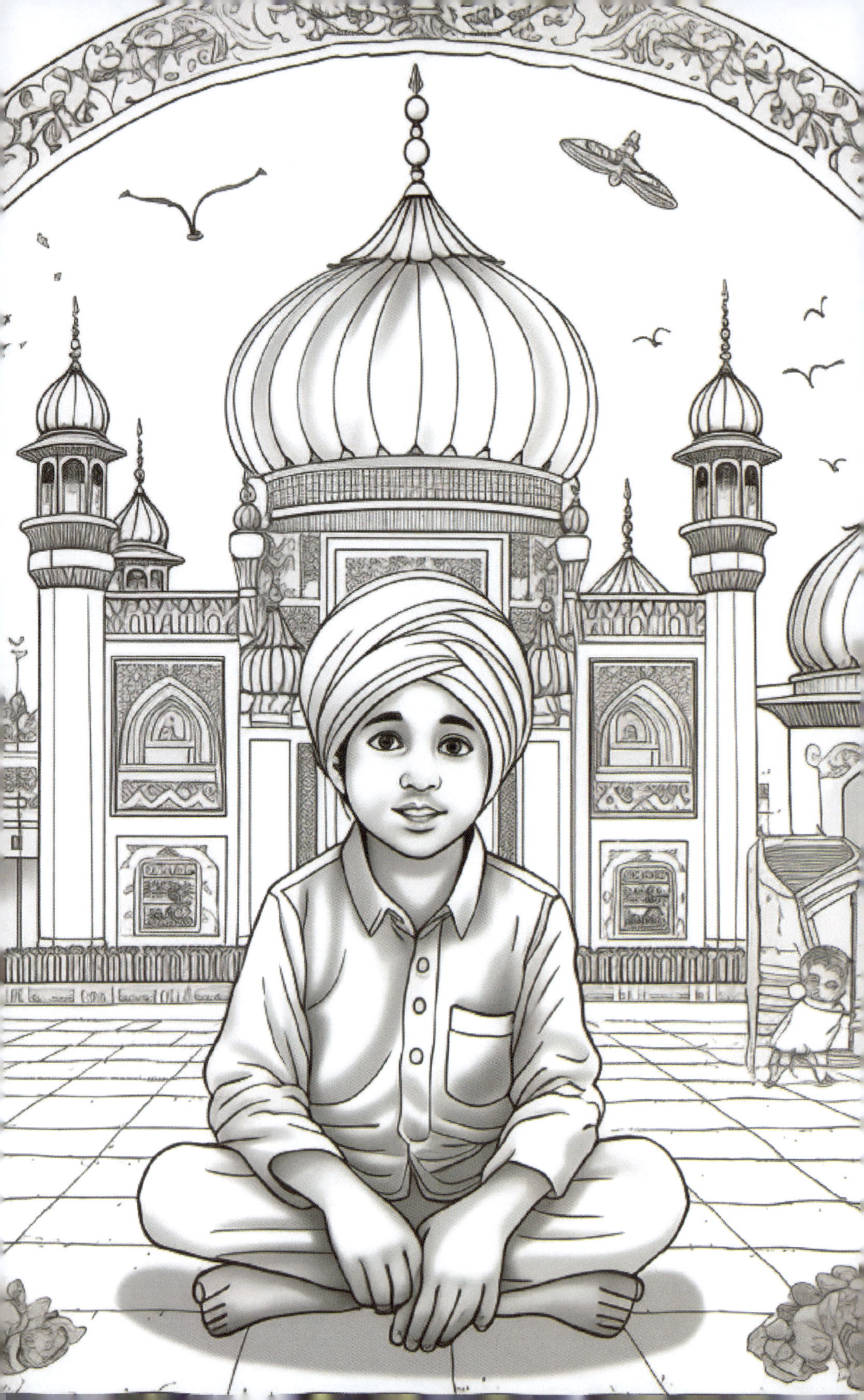

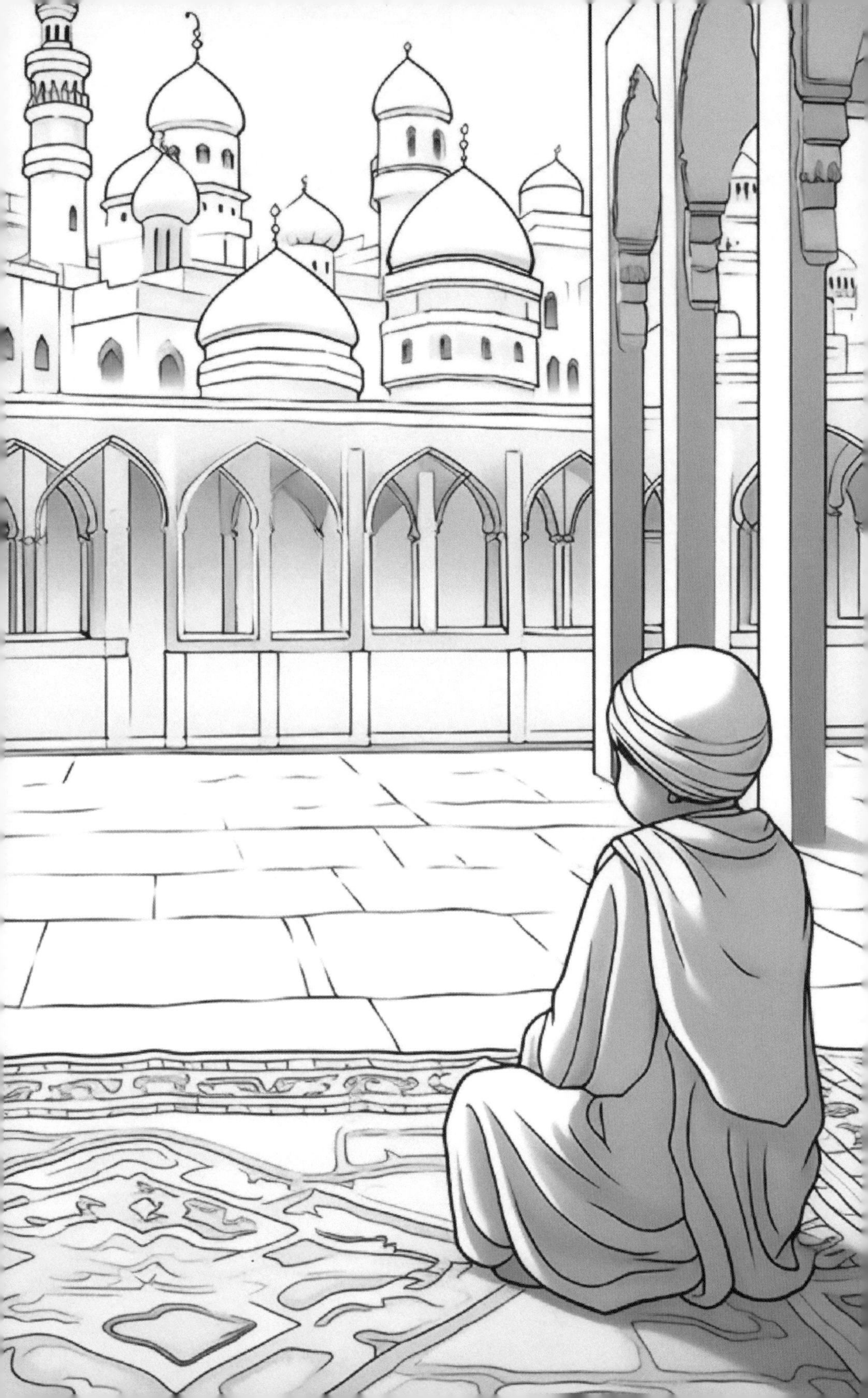

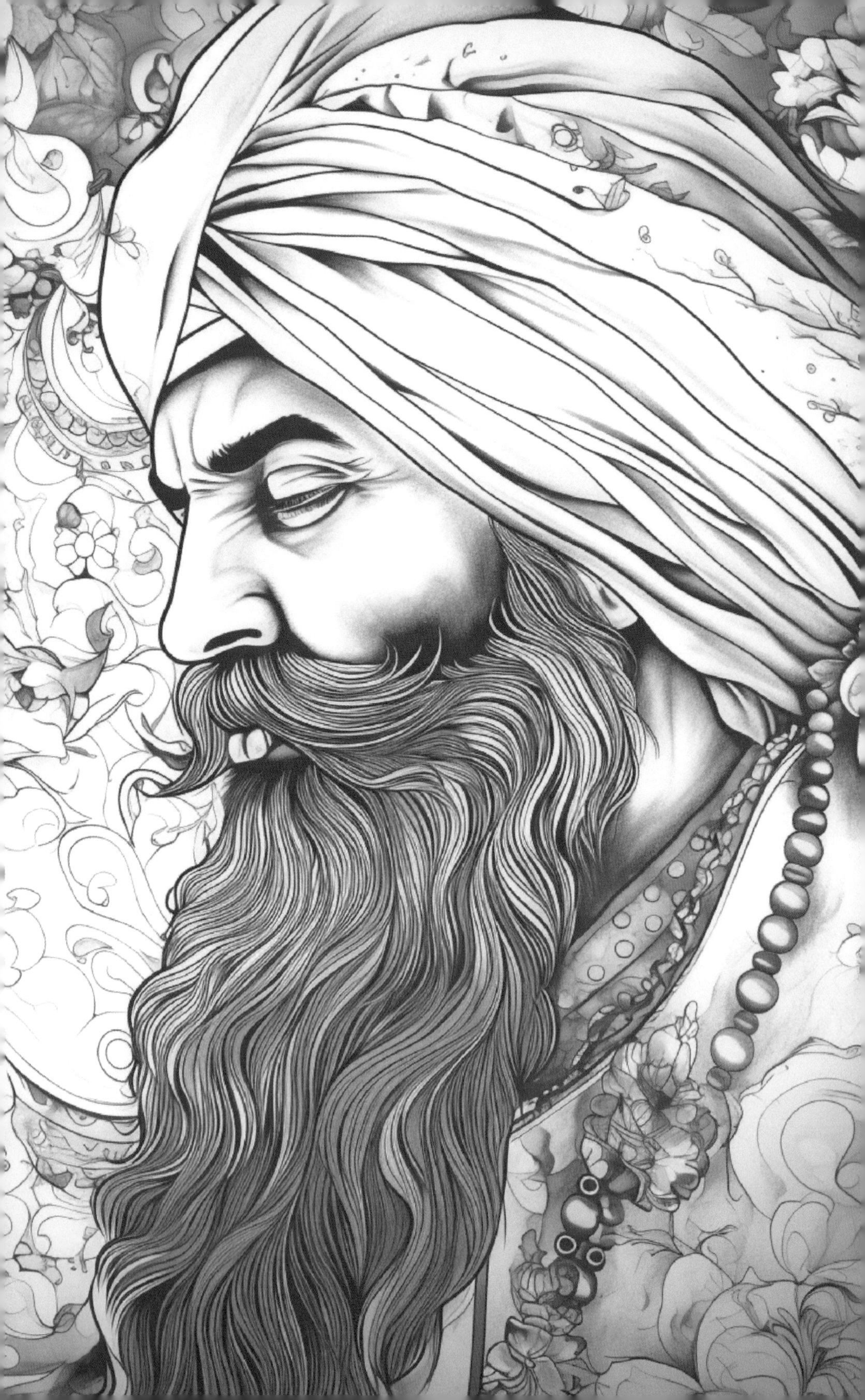

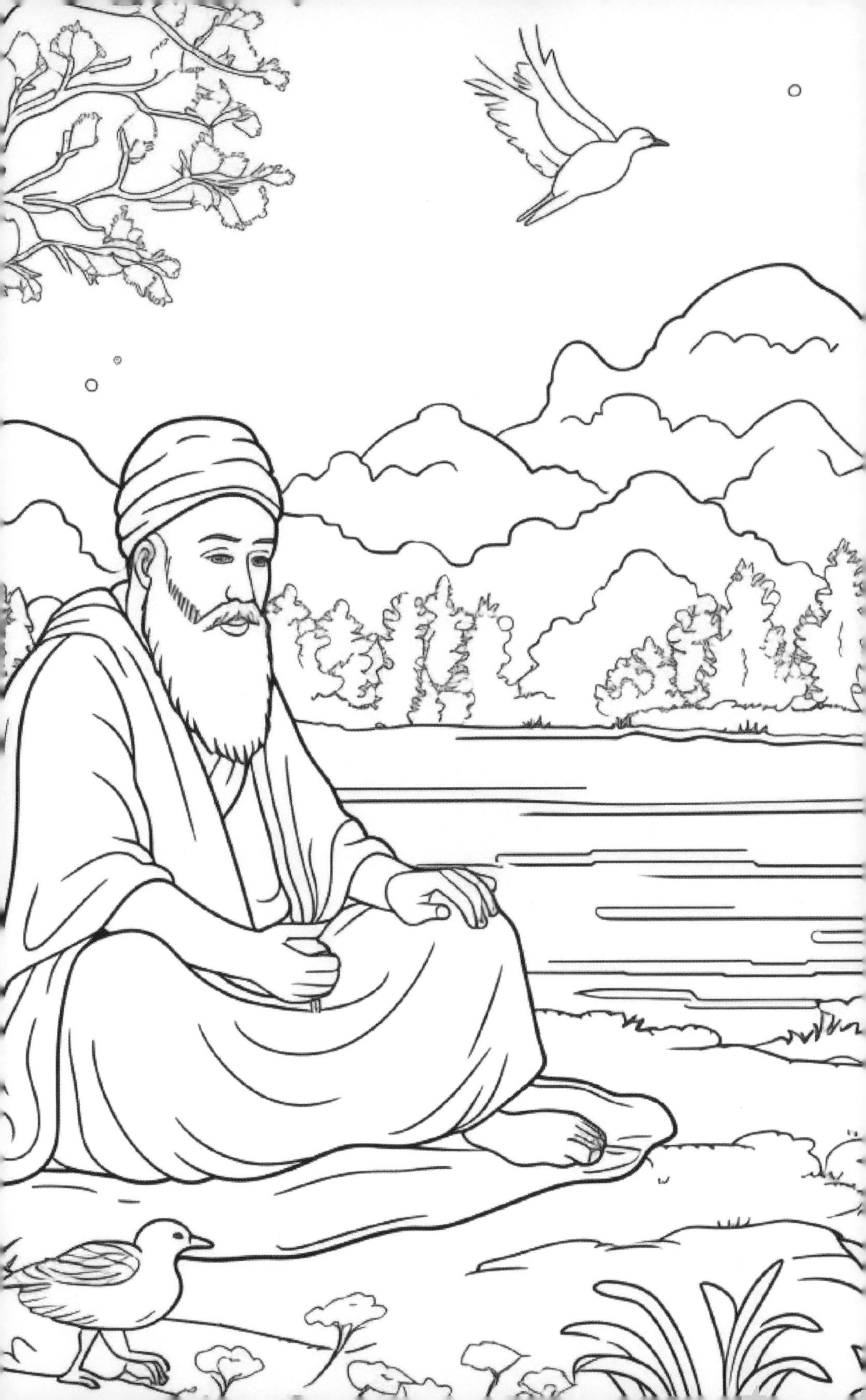

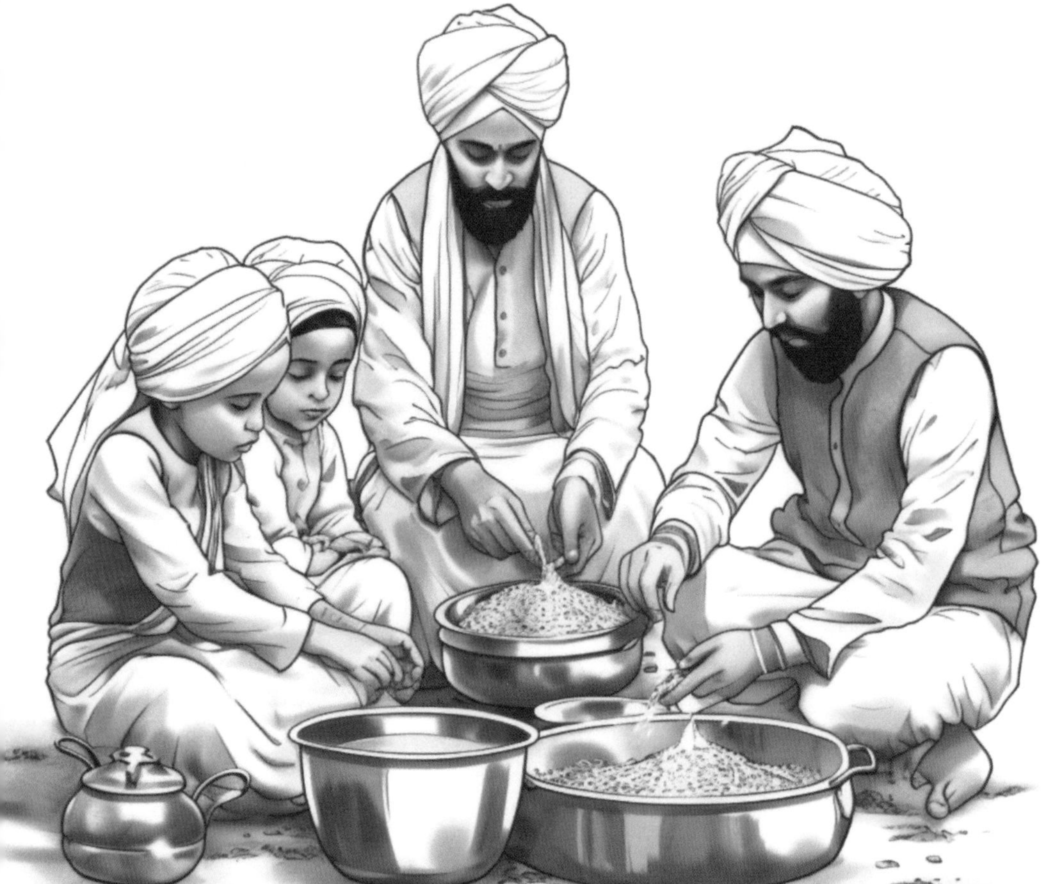

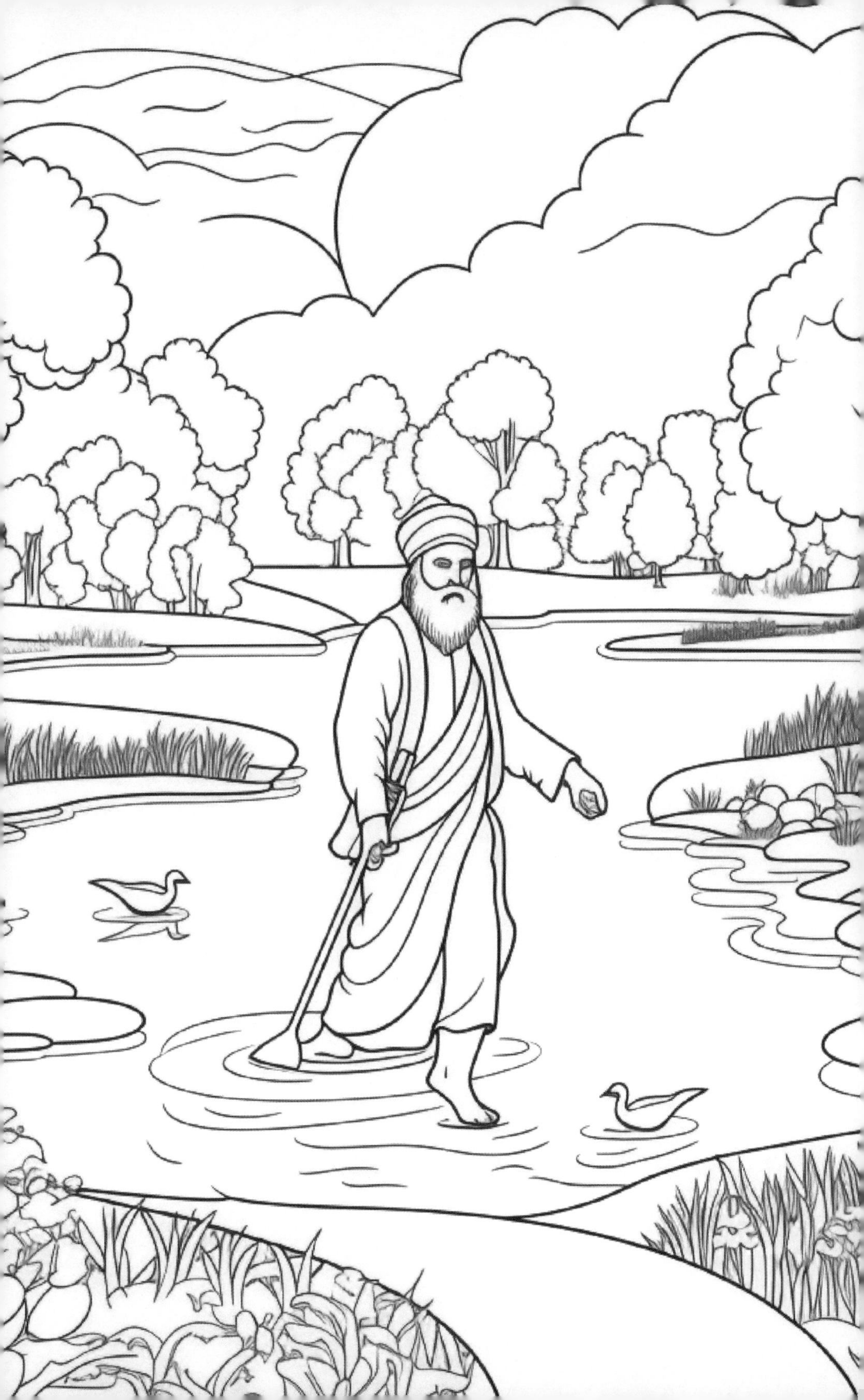

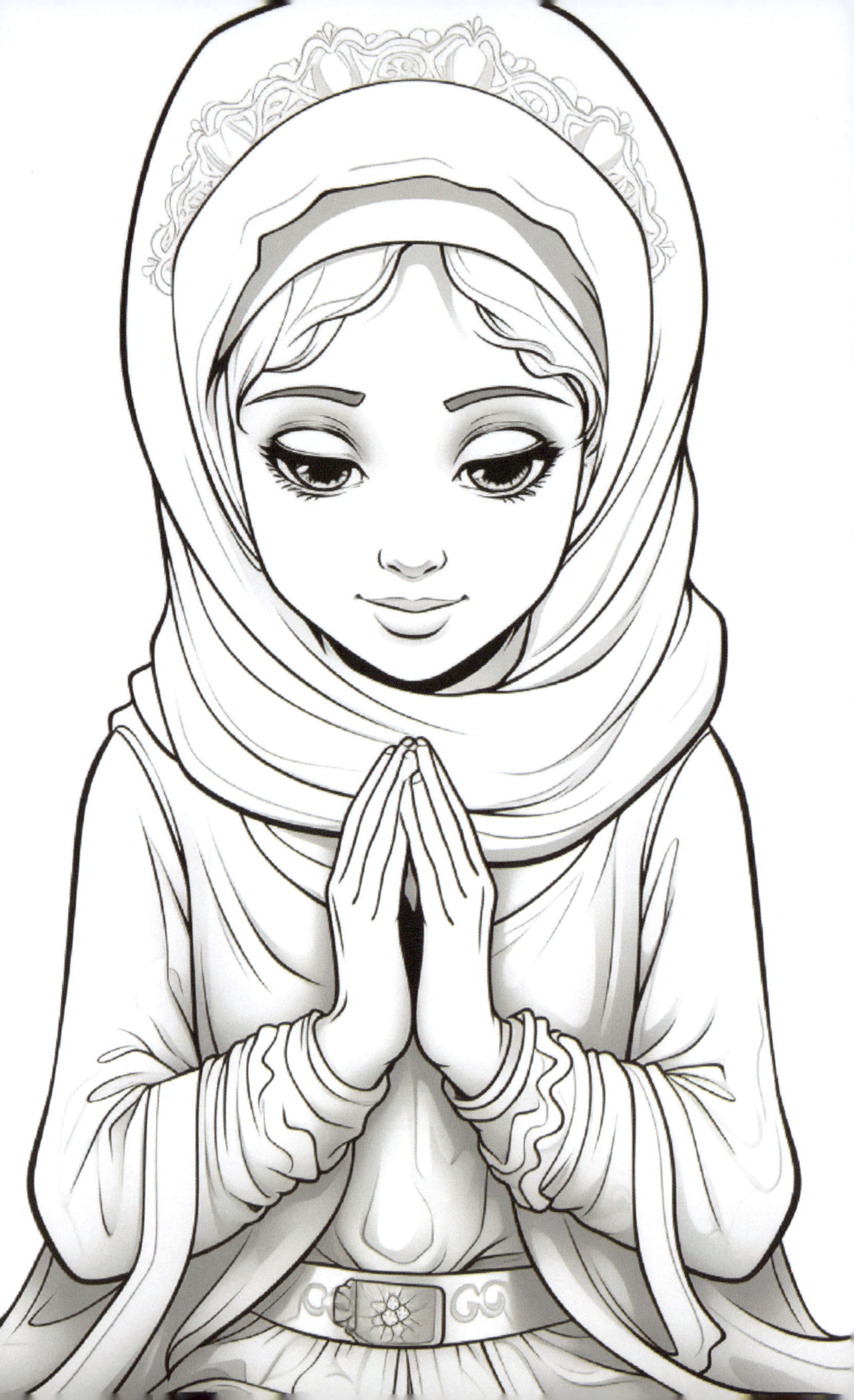

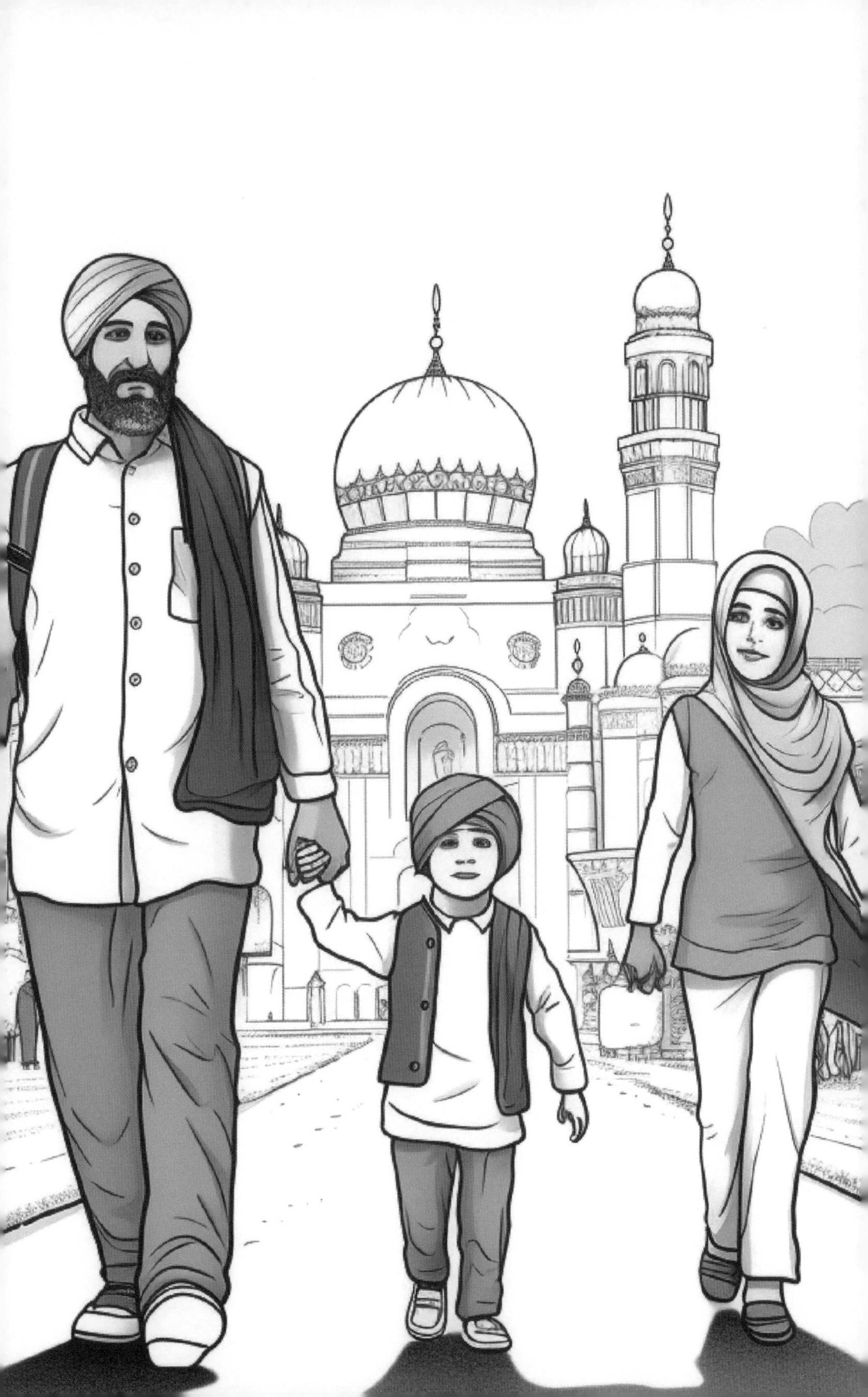

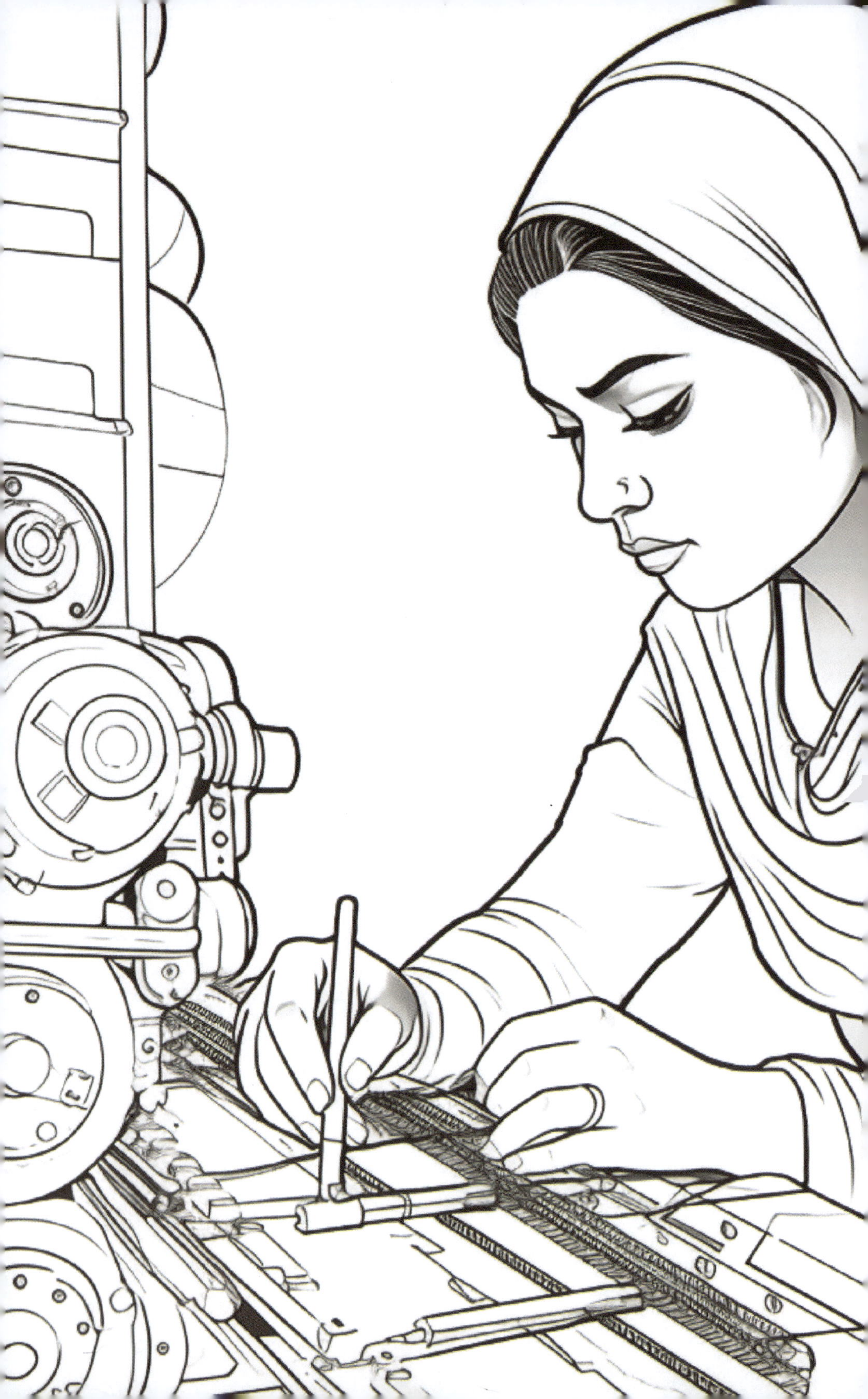

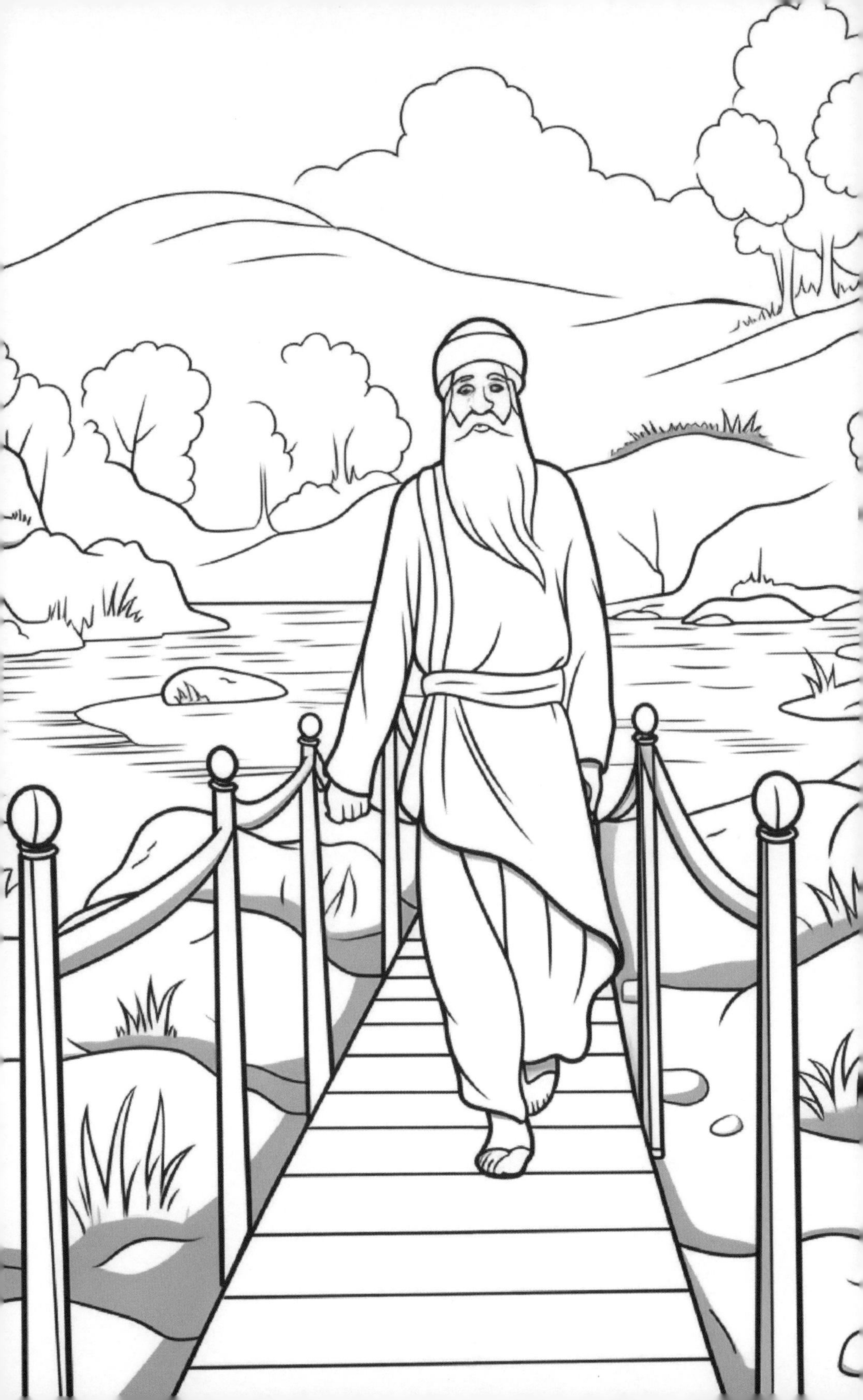

DRAW YOUR FAVOURITE GURU

DRAW YOUR FAVOURITE GURU

WAHEGURU JI KA KHALSA, WAHEGURU JI KI FATEH!

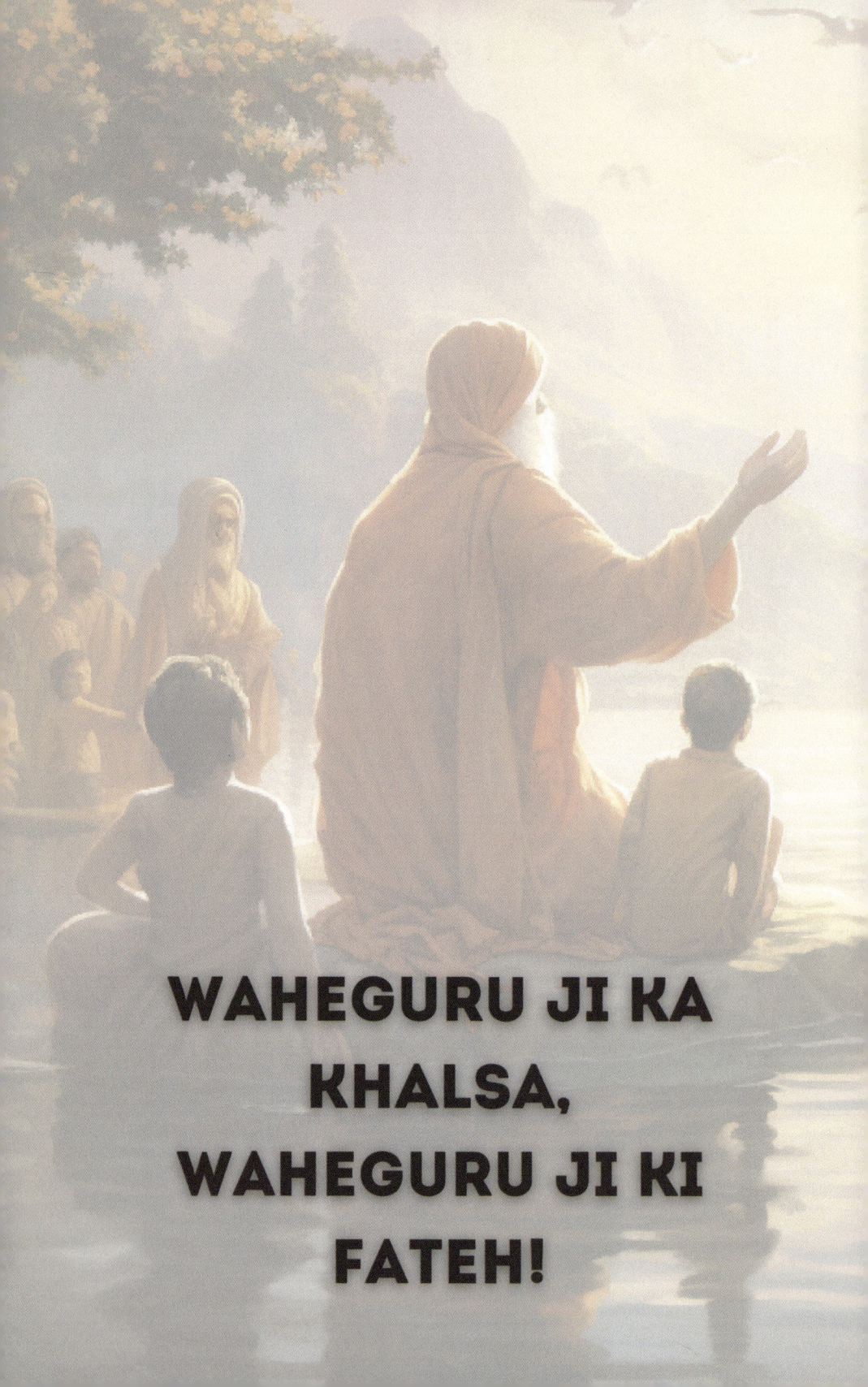

Dear Esteemed Readers,

I want to express my heartfelt gratitude for embarking on this enlightening journey through the profound teachings of the 10 Sikh Gurus. Crafting this book was a labor of love, and I sincerely hope it has ignited inspiration and motivation within your hearts.

However, our voyage doesn't end here. This book merely marks the commencement of our "Unlock the Hidden Wisdom" series, where we delve into deeper teachings from the rich tapestry of ancient Indian sources.

Your support and engagement mean the world to me. If this book has touched your spirit and kindled the flames of curiosity and learning, I kindly invite you to share your thoughts by leaving a review. Your feedback is a beacon that guides us in our mission to inspire young minds.

Moreover, I encourage you to explore our other literary treasures within the series: "Sikhi for the Young Minds." These volumes offer a captivating gateway into the world of Sikhism and the teachings of the revered Sikh Gurus. It's a powerful tool to instill inspiration and motivation in the hearts and minds of children, nurturing their souls with wisdom and compassion.

Stay connected with us on social media @manifestbyai. We welcome your thoughts, questions, and shared journeys of wisdom.

With profound gratitude and warm regards,

MS Chadha

Printed in Great Britain
by Amazon